FURTHER ALONG
The Road Less Traveled

D0030040

Also by M. Scott Peck, M.D., available in Large Print from Walker and Company

The Road Less Traveled: A New Psychology of Love, Traditional Values and Spiritual Growth

FURTHER ALONG
The Road Less Traveled

The Unending Journey
Toward Spiritual Growth

THE EDITED LECTURES

M. SCOTT PECK, M.D.

WALKER AND COMPANY
New York

Large Print edition published by arrangement with Simon & Schuster, Inc., 1994.

Large Print edition published simultaneously in Canada by Thomas Allen & Son Canada, Limited, Markham, Ontario.

Library of Congress Cataloging-in-Publication Data
Peck, M. Scott (Morgan Scott). 1936–
    Further along the road less traveled : the unending journey toward spiritual growth : the edited lectures / M. Scott Peck, M.D. — 1st large print ed.
        p.   cm.
ISBN 0-8027-2682-8
1. Self-actualization (Psychology)—Religious aspects—Christianity. 2. Maturation (Psychology)—Religious aspects—Christianity. 3. Interpersonal relations—Religious aspects—Christianity. 4. Spiritual life.   I. Title.
[BV4598.2.P43   1994]
158′.1—dc20   94-33203
                                                                                CIP

Names and identifying characteristics of certain individuals portrayed in this book have been changed to protect their identities. The author is grateful for permission to reprint excerpts from the following material: Reverence for Life, *by Albert Schweitzer. Copyright © 1969 by Rhena Eckert-Schweitzer. Used by permission of HarperCollins Publishers, Inc.;* John of the Cross, Selected Writings, *ed. by Kieran Kavanaugh, O. C. D. Translated from the Spanish by Kieran Kavanaugh, O. C. D. © 1987 by Kieran Kavanaugh, O. C. D. Used by permission of Paulist Press;* Evolution of Physics, *by Albert Einstein and Leopold Infeld. Copyright © 1938 by Albert Einstein and Leopold Infeld. Copyright renewed © 1966 by Albert Einstein and Leopold Infeld. Reprinted by permission of Simon & Schuster, Inc.*

First Large Print Edition, 1994
Walker and Company
435 Hudson Street
New York, New York 10014

Printed in the United States of America
10 9 8 7 6 5 4 3 2 1

TO
all who have been,
one way or another,
my "audience";
thank you
for listening

Contents

Acknowledgments   ix
Introduction   xi

PART ONE
THE FIRST STEP: GROWING UP

ONE   Consciousness and the Problem of Pain   3
TWO   Blame and Forgiveness   17
THREE   The Issue of Death and Meaning   38
FOUR   The Taste for Mystery   64

PART TWO
THE NEXT STEP: KNOWING YOUR SELF

FIVE   Self-Love versus Self-Esteem   83
SIX   Mythology and Human Nature   98
SEVEN   Spirituality and Human Nature   115
EIGHT   Addiction: The Sacred Disease   138

PART THREE
THE ULTIMATE STEP:
IN SEARCH OF A PERSONAL GOD

NINE	The Role of Religion in Spiritual Growth	159
TEN	Matter and Spirit	185
ELEVEN	New Age: Symboline or Diaboline?	207
TWELVE	Sexuality and Spirituality	236
	Epilogue: Psychiatry's Predicament	251

Acknowledgments

T here are two ways to edit a collection of lectures: the easy way and the hard way.

The easy way is to simply transcribe audiotapes, correct the grammar, and print them, even though the result might appear to be a hodgepodge of unrelated subjects. The hard way is to try to take these disparate subjects and, weaving in new material, create an imaginative, unified, and easily readable whole.

Simon & Schuster and I elected this latter course, and I have spent countless hours meeting with my editors to reorganize and integrate my lectures, and to give them new material and answer their questions to fill in any gaps. I have also done extensive editing of the resulting manuscript to impart the flavor of my thinking. This book is very much my own creation, and I am pleased with it.

But is also a co-creation and would simply not have been possible without the immense editorial assistance of Simon & Schuster. My several hundred hours spent on this project have been matched in triplicate by the staff of Simon & Schuster, including multiple typists, copy editors, and fact checkers. I am grateful to them all.

But I need to single out three people for special mention. One is Ursula Obst, who more than anyone else was responsible over the course of many months for the creative artistry of weaving a collection of assorted lectures into a coherent, very real book.

I also wish to express my gratitude to Burton Beals, who line edited Ursula's product in preparation for my own editing. Through his laborious efforts and many conversations with me, the whole has become, I believe, highly readable.

Finally, I would like to thank Fred Hills, my long-time editor at Simon & Schuster. The book was his idea. It has been his brainchild, and he has patiently shepherded it for two years, from start to finish. He was its instigator and coordinator and provider, and it simply could not have occurred without him.

Introduction

Y ou may remember that *The Road Less Traveled* opened with the sentence "Life is difficult." And to that great truth, I will now add another translation:

Life is complex.

Each one of us must make his own path through life. There are no self-help manuals, no formulas, no easy answers. The right road for one is the wrong road for another. Nowhere in this book will you find it said: "Go this way," "Make a left turn here." The journey of life is not paved in blacktop; it is not brightly lit, and it has no road signs. It is a rocky path through the wilderness.

In this book, I will endeavor to put down some of the things I have learned in the past ten years which have eased my way as I groped through the wilderness. But if I tell you that when I lost my way, I found it again by following the moss growing on the north side of trees, I will almost certainly have to warn you that in the redwood forests there are many trees covered with moss on all sides.

I also caution you not to interpret the word "further" in the title or anything else in this book as suggesting that the road is linear—that you take one step after another in a straightforward progression. Although "further" might sound as if I am saying, "Here's where Scott Peck was, here's where Scott Peck is now, and if you are here, then this is where you will likely be next year," that is not what I intend to imply. That's not what the road is like. It is, rather, like a series of concentric circles expanding out from the core, and there is nothing simple or straightforward about it.

But we do not have to make the journey alone. We can ask help of the force in our lives that we recognize to be greater than we are. A force that we all see differently, but of whose presence most of us are aware. And as we make our way, we can help each other.

If this book aids you in any way, I hope, most of all, that it will assist you to think less simplistically. I hope you will abandon the urge to simplify everything, to look for formulas and easy answers, and begin to think multidimensionally, to glory in the mystery and paradoxes of life, not to be dismayed by the multitude of causes and consequences that are inherent in each experience—to appreciate the fact that life is complex.

PART ONE

The First Step: Growing Up

CHAPTER ONE

Consciousness and the Problem of Pain

All my life I used to wonder what I would become when I grew up. Then, about seven years ago, I realized that I never was going to grow up—that growing is an ever ongoing process. So I asked myself, "Well, Scotty, what is it that you've become thus far?" And as soon as I asked that question, I realized, to my absolute horror, that what I have become is an evangelist. An evangelist is the last thing on earth I ever thought I would become. And it's probably the last thing on earth you ever wanted to encounter.

The word "evangelist" carries the worst possible associations and probably brings to your mind the image of a manicured and coiffed preacher in a two-thousand-dollar suit, his gold-ringed fingers gripping a leatherette-covered Bible as he shouts at the top of his lungs: "Save me, Jee-sus!"

Fear not. I don't mean to suggest that I have become that kind of evangelist. I am using the word "evangelist" in its original sense—the bringer of good news. But I must warn you, I am also the bringer of bad news. I am an evangelist who brings good news and bad news.

If you are anything like me, you are into delaying

gratification, so when you are asked, "Which do you want first, the good news or the bad news?" you answer, "Well, the bad news first, please." So let me get the bad news over with: I don't know anything.

It might seem odd that an evangelist, a "bringer of truth," would confess so readily that he doesn't know anything. But the real truth of the matter is that you don't know anything either. None of us does. We dwell in a profoundly mysterious universe.

Evangelists are also supposed to bring "glad tidings of comfort and joy." The other piece of bad news is that I am going to be talking about the journey through life, and in so doing I cannot avoid talking about pain. Pain is simply a part of being human and it has been so since the Garden of Eden.

The story of the Garden of Eden is, of course, a myth. But like other myths, it is an embodiment of truth. And among the many truthful things the myth of the Garden of Eden tells us is how we human beings evolved into consciousness.

When we ate the apple from the Tree of the Knowledge of Good and Evil, we became conscious, and having become conscious, we immediately became self-conscious. That was how God recognized that we had eaten the apple—we were suddenly modest and shy. So one of the things this myth tells us is that it is human to be shy.

I have had the opportunity, through my career as a psychiatrist and more recently as an author and lecturer, to meet a great number of wonderful, deep-thinking people, and I have never met such a person who was not basically shy. A few of them had not thought of themselves as shy, but as we talked about it, they came to

4

realize that they were in fact shy. And the very few people I have met who were not shy were people who had been damaged in some way, who had lost some of their humanity.

It is human to be shy, and we became shy in the Garden of Eden when we became self-conscious. When this happened to us, we became conscious of ourselves as separate entities. We lost that sense of oneness with nature, with the rest of the universe. And this loss of the sense of oneness with the rest of creation is symbolized by our banishment from Paradise.

GROWING UP PAINFULLY

When we were banished from Paradise, we were banished forever. We can never go back to Eden. If you remember the story, the way is barred by cherubims and a flaming sword.

We cannot go back. We can only go forward.

To go back to Eden would be like trying to return to our mother's womb, to infancy. Since we cannot go back to the womb or infancy, we must grow up. We can only go forward through the desert of life, making our way painfully over parched and barren ground into increasingly deeper levels of consciousness.

This is an extremely important truth because a great deal of human psychopathology, including the abuse of drugs, arises out of the attempt to get back to Eden. At cocktail parties we tend to need at least that one drink to help diminish our self-consciousness, to diminish our shyness. It works, right? And if we get just the right amount of alcohol or just the right amount of pot or coke or some combination thereof, for a few minutes or a few hours we may regain temporarily that lost sense of one-ness with the universe. We may recapture that deliciously warm and fuzzy sense of being one with nature once again.

Of course, the feeling never lasts very long and the price usually isn't worth it. So the myth is true. We really cannot go back to Eden. We must go forward through the desert. But that journey is hard and consciousness often painful. And so most people stop their journey as quickly as they can. They find what looks like a safe place, burrow into the sand, and stay there rather than go forward through the painful desert, which is filled with cactuses and thorns and sharp rocks.

Even if most people have been taught at one time or another that "those things that hurt, instruct" (to borrow Benjamin Franklin's phrase), the education of the desert is so painful that they discontinue it as early as they can.

Senility is not just a biological disorder. It can also be a manifestation of a refusal to grow up, a psychological disorder preventable by anyone who embarks on a lifetime pattern of psychospiritual growth. Those who stop learning and growing early in their lives and stop changing and become fixed often lapse into what is sometimes called their "second childhood." They become whiny and demanding and self-centered. But this isn't because they have entered their second childhood. They have never left their first, and the veneer of adulthood is worn thin, revealing the emotional child that lurks underneath.

We psychotherapists know that most people who look like adults are actually emotional children walking around in adult's clothing. And we know this *not* because the people that come to us are more immature than most. On the contrary, those who come to psychotherapy with genuine intent to grow are those relative few who are called out of immaturity, who are no longer willing to tolerate their own childishness, although they may not yet see the way out. The rest of the population never manages to fully grow up, and perhaps it is for this reason that they hate so to talk about growing old.

Back in January of 1980, soon after I wrote *The Road Less Traveled*, which in many ways is a book about growing up, I was being driven around to a number of TV and radio stations on a promotional tour by a cabdriver in Washington, D.C. After the second or third station, he said, "Hey man, whatja doin'?"

So I told him that I was promoting a book, and he asked, "What's it about?"

I went into this intellectual bit about how it was an integration of psychiatry and religion. After about thirty seconds he commented, "Well, it sounds to me like it's about getting your shit together."

That man had the gift of discernment. So at the next TV talk show I went to, I asked if I could tell that story.

They said no. Thinking that they objected to the word "shit," I offered to say "stuff" instead. But they still said no.

People just don't want to talk about real maturation. It is too painful.

CONSTRUCTIVE SUFFERING

If I am willing to talk about pain, it does not mean I am some kind of masochist. On the contrary. I see absolutely no virtue whatsoever in unconstructive suffering. If I have a headache, the very first thing I do is go to the kitchen and get myself two superstrength, uncapsulized

Tylenols. I see absolutely no virtue in an ordinary tension headache.

But there is such a thing as *constructive* suffering. And the difference between unconstructive suffering and constructive suffering is one of the most important things to learn in dealing with the pain of growing up. Unconstructive suffering, like headaches, is something you ought to get rid of. Constructive suffering you ought to bear and work through.

I prefer to use the terms "neurotic suffering" and "existential suffering," and here is an example of how I make that distinction. You may remember that about forty years ago, when Freud's theories first filtered down to the intelligentsia and were misinterpreted—as so often happens—there was a whole bunch of avant-garde parents who, having learned that guilt feelings could have something to do with neuroses, resolved that they were going to raise guilt-free children. What an awful thing to try to do to a child!

Our jails are filled with people who are there precisely because they do not have any guilt, or do not have enough guilt. We need a certain amount of guilt in order to exist in society. And that's what I call existential guilt.

I hasten to stress, however, that too much guilt, rather than enhancing our existence, impedes it. This is neurotic guilt. It is like walking around a golf course with eighty-seven clubs in your bag instead of fourteen, which is the number needed to play optimal golf. It's just so much excess baggage, and you ought to get rid of it as quickly as possible. If that means going into psychotherapy, then you should do that. Neurotic guilt is unnecessary, and it only impedes your journey through the desert.

This is true not only of guilt, but also of other forms of emotional suffering, like anxiety, for example, which can be either existential or neurotic. And the trick is to determine which is which.

There is a very simple albeit brutal rule for dealing with the emotional pain and suffering of life. It's a three-step process.

First, whenever you are suffering emotionally, ask yourself: "Is my suffering—my anxiety or my guilt—existential or is it neurotic? Is this pain enhancing my existence or is it limiting it?" Now perhaps about ten percent of the time, you really won't be able to answer that question. But about ninety percent of the time, if you can think to ask it, the answer will be very clear. If, for example, you are anxious about filing your income taxes on time because you once got hit with a big late-payment penalty, I can assure you that the anxiety you feel is existential. It's appropriate. Go with your anxiety and file on time. On the other hand, if you determine that the suffering you are experiencing is neurotic and is impeding your existence, then the second step is to ask yourself: "How would I behave if I did not have this anxiety or guilt?"

And the third step is to behave that way. As Alcoholics Anonymous teaches: "Act as if," or "Fake it to make it."

The way I first came to learn about this rule was in dealing with my own shyness. It is human to be shy, but we can deal with it in ways that are either neurotic or existential. In the audience, listening to famous speakers, I sometimes felt there was a question I should ask them, some piece of information I wanted to know, or some comment I wanted to make —in public, or even in private after the speech. But I would hold back because I was too shy and afraid of being rejected or of looking like a fool.

After a while, I finally came to ask myself: "Is this way of dealing with your shyness—which is holding you back from asking questions—enhancing your existence or is it limiting it?" As soon as I asked that, it was clear that it was limiting my existence. And then I said to myself: "Well, Scotty, how would you behave if you weren't so shy? How would you behave if you were the Queen of England or President of the United States?" The answer was clear that I would approach the speaker and have my say. So then I told myself: "Okay, then, go ahead and behave that way. Fake it to make it. Act as if you weren't shy."

I admit that is a scary thing to do, but this is where courage comes in. One of the things that never cease to amaze me is how relatively few people understand what courage is. Most people think that courage is the absence of fear. The absence of fear is not courage; the absence of fear is some kind of brain damage. Courage is the capacity to go ahead in spite of the fear, or in spite of the pain. When you do that, you will find that overcoming that fear will not only make you stronger but will be a big step forward toward maturity.

Just what is maturity? When I wrote *The Road Less Traveled*, although I described a number of immature people, I never gave a definition of maturity. But it seems to me what characterizes most immature people is that they sit around complaining that life doesn't meet their demands. As Richard Bach wrote in *Illusions*, "Argue for your limitations, and sure enough they are yours." But what characterizes those relative few who

10

are fully mature is that they regard it as their responsibility—even as an opportunity—to meet life's demands.

CONSCIOUSNESS AND HEALING

To proceed very far through the desert, you must be willing to meet existential suffering and work it through. In order to do that, if you are like most of us, you need to change your attitude toward pain in one way or another. And here is some good news. The quickest way to change your attitude toward pain is to accept the fact that everything that happens to us has been designed for our spiritual growth.

Donald Nichol, the author of *Holiness*, refers to it in his introduction as a how-to book. He says if you're caught carrying around a book on the subject of holiness and people ask you what you are doing with it, you're likely to tell them, "Well, I'm simply interested in what authorities have to say about the subject." Actually, Nichol points out, there's absolutely no reason for you to purchase or borrow, much less carry around a book on the subject of holiness unless you want to be holy. And so he calls it a how-to book, about how to be holy. Approximately two thirds of the way through that book there's a wonderful sentence where Nichol says, "We cannot lose once we realize that everything that happens to us has been designed to teach us holiness."

Now what better news can there be than that we cannot lose, we are bound to win? We are guaranteed winners once we simply realize that everything that happens to us has been designed to teach us what we need to know on our journey.

The problem, however, is that this realization re-

11

quires a complete shift in our attitude toward pain—and, I think, toward consciousness. Remember in the story of the Garden of Eden, we became conscious when we ate the apple from the Tree of the Knowledge of Good and Evil. Consciousness then became for us both the cause of our pain and the cause of our salvation, which is a word synonymous with healing.

Consciousness is the cause of our pain because, of course, were we not conscious, we would not feel pain. One of the things that we do for people to spare them unconstructive, unnecessary suffering—physical suffering—is to give them anesthesia so that they can lose consciousness and not feel the pain.

But while consciousness is the whole cause of pain, it is also the cause of our salvation, because salvation is the process of becoming increasingly conscious. When we become increasingly conscious, we go further and further into the desert instead of burrowing into a hole like the people who choose not to grow up. And as we travel onward, we bear more and more pain—because of our very consciousness.

As I said above, the word *salvation* means "healing." It comes from the same word as *salve*, which you put on your skin in order to heal an area of irritation or infection. Salvation is the process of healing and the process of becoming whole. And health, wholeness, and holiness are all derived from the same root. They all mean virtually the same thing.

Even old atheist Sigmund Freud recognized the relationship between healing and consciousness when he said that the purpose of psychotherapy—healing of the psyche—was to make the unconscious conscious; that is, to increase consciousness. Carl Jung further helped us understand the unconscious, ascribing evil to our refusal to meet our shadow, or that part of our personality that we like to deny, that we like not to think about, not to be conscious of, that we're continually trying to sweep under the rug of consciousness and keep unconscious.

Note that Jung ascribed human evil not to the shadow itself but to the *refusal* to meet this shadow. And refusal is a very active term. Those people who are evil are not just passively unconscious or ignorant; they will go far out of their way to remain ignorant or unconscious; they will kill or start wars to do so.

I recognize, of course, that evil—like Love or God or Truth—is too large to submit to any single adequate definition. But one of the better definitions for evil is that it is "militant ignorance." Militant unconsciousness.

The Vietnam War is one of the best examples I know of this militant ignorance on a grand scale. When the evidence first began to accumulate in 1963 or 1964 that our policies in Indochina weren't working, our first response was to deny that anything was wrong. We said we just needed a couple more million dollars and a few more special forces. But then the evidence continued to accumulate—our policies clearly weren't working. So what happened then? We sent in more troops, the body count began to escalate, and incidents of brutality became commonplace. It was the time of My Lai. Then as the evidence continued to pour in, we continued to ignore it. Instead, we bombed Cambodia and started talking about peace with honor.

Even today, despite all that we now know, some Americans continue to think that we succeeded in bargaining our way out of Vietnam. We didn't bargain our way out of Vietnam—we were defeated. But somehow many still refuse to see this.

OASES IN THE DESERT

Consciousness brings more pain, but it also brings more joy. Because as you go further into the desert—if you go far enough—you will begin to discover little patches of green, little oases that you had never seen before. And if you go still further, you may even discover some streams of living water underneath the sand, or if you go still further, you may even be able to fulfill your own ultimate destiny.

Now if you doubt me, consider the example of a man who went on the journey far into the desert. He was the poet T. S. Eliot, who became famous early on in his career for writing poems of total aridity and despair. In the first, "The Love Song of J. Alfred Prufrock," which he published in 1917 at age twenty-nine, he wrote:

I grow old. . . . I grow old . . .
I shall wear the bottoms of my trousers rolled.

Shall I part my hair behind? Do I dare to eat a peach?
I shall wear white flannel trousers, and walk upon
    the beach.
I have heard the mermaids singing, each to each.

I do not think that they will sing to me.

It is important to keep in mind that J. Alfred Prufrock of the poem lived—as did T. S. Eliot—in a world of high society, the ultimate civilized world, yet he lived in a

14

spiritual wasteland. Not surprisingly then, five years later, Eliot published a poem called "The Waste Land." And in this poem, he actually focused on the desert. It is also a poem that has in it a great deal of aridity and despair, but for the first time in Eliot's poetry there are little patches of green, little hints of vegetation here and there, images of water, and of shadow under rocks.

Then in his late forties and early fifties, Eliot wrote poems like "Four Quartets," the first of which opens with references to a rose garden, birds calling and children laughing. And he went on to write some of the richest and most luxuriously verdant, and mystical poetry that has ever been written, and, indeed, he is reputed to have ended his life very joyfully.

There is much solace we could take from Eliot's example as we ourselves struggle along with our rocky path and our pain. We need some comfort on our journey, but one of the things we don't need is quick fixes. I have seen a lot of people who literally murder each other with quick fixes in the name of healing.

They do this for very self-centered reasons. For example, let's say that Rick is my friend and he is in pain. Because he is my friend, that causes me pain, but I don't like to feel pain. So what I'd like to do is to heal Rick as quickly as I possibly can to get rid of my pain. I'd like to give him some kind of easy answer like: "Oh, I'm sorry your mother died but don't feel bad about it. She's gone to Heaven." Or: "Gee, I had that problem once and all you have to do is go running."

But more often than not, the most healing thing that we can do with someone who is in pain, rather than trying to get rid of that pain, is to sit there and be willing to share it. We have to learn to hear and to bear other people's pain. That is all part of becoming more conscious. And the more conscious we become, the more we see the games that other people play and their sins and manipulations, but we're also more conscious of their burdens and their sorrows.

As we grow spiritually, we can take on more and more of other people's pain, and then the most amazing thing happens. The more pain you are willing to take on, the more joy you will also begin to feel. And this is truly good news of what makes the journey ultimately so worthwhile.

CHAPTER TWO

Blame and Forgiveness

A big part of growing up is learning to forgive. We go through life blaming others for our pain. And blame always begins with anger.

Anger is a powerful emotion that originates in the brain. Throughout the human brain there are little collections of nerve cells called neural centers. And in that part of the brain which we call the midbrain, these centers are involved in the governance and in the production of emotions. Neurosurgeons have actually mapped out the locations of these centers. With a human being lying on an operating table under local anesthesia, they insert electrodes, or very fine needles, into the brain from the tip of which they can deliver a millivolt of current.

For instance, we have a euphoria center, and if neurosurgeons insert the needle in that area and deliver a millivolt of current, the patient lying on the table will say, "Oh wow! You doctors sure are wonderful and this is such a marvelous hospital. Do it again, will you?" This feeling of euphoria is very powerful, and the reason certain drugs like heroin are so habituating is that they may have a stimulating effect upon our euphoria center.

Studies have been done on rats in which neurosurgeons insert an electrode into a rat's euphoria center and allow the rat to stimulate itself by pressing a lever. As a result, the rat will be so busy pressing the lever that it will not eat and will starve to death. It will pleasure itself to death!

Not far away from the euphoria center, there is another center which governs a quite different emotion—the depression center. If neurosurgeons insert an electrode in that center and give it a millivolt of current, the patient lying on the table will say, "Oh God, everything looks gray, I feel horrible, I feel just awful. Please, please stop it." Similarly, there is an anger center. And if neurosurgeons stimulate that, they had better have the patient strapped down on the table.

These centers have been built into the human brain through millions of years of evolution, and they are there for a purpose. For example, if you somehow cut out the anger center in a child's brain so that she could not get angry, you would have a very passive child. But what do you think would happen to such a passive child when she got into kindergarten or first or second grade? She would be stomped on, she would be walked right over, she might even get killed. Anger serves a purpose; we need it for our very survival. It's not bad in itself.

The anger center in human beings works in exactly the same way as it does in other creatures. It is basically a territorial mechanism, firing off when any other creature impinges upon our territory. We are no different from a dog fighting another dog that wanders into its territory, except that for us human beings, our definitions of territory are much more complex. Not only do we have a geographical territory and become angry when someone comes uninvited onto our property and starts picking our flowers, but we also have a psychological territory, and we become angry whenever anyone criticizes us. We also have a theological or an ideological territory, and we tend to become angry whenever anyone criticizes our beliefs or casts aspersions upon our ideas.

Because our human territory is so complex and multifaceted, our anger center is firing off all the time, and often very inappropriately. To give you an idea of how inappropriately, sometimes it can fire off even when we invite people into our territory.

Back some twenty-five years ago when I went into analysis, I already had an interest in the relationship between psychology and spirituality, and knowing that Carl Jung had stressed this area, I went to great trouble to find a Jungian therapist. I went to see him, and I kept waiting for him to say something Jungian to me. The only problem was that he approached me like a Freudian, which, as I later learned, was exactly the way I needed to be treated.

After our introduction, this therapist didn't say a word for the next seven sessions. He made me do all the talking and I began to get more and more annoyed with him. Here I was paying him the vast sum (back then) of twenty-five dollars an hour, and he wasn't doing or saying anything to earn his money. Finally, during the ninth session as I was talking about how I felt about a particular matter, he actually said something. He said, "Well, I'm not quite sure I understand yet why you feel that way." And I snapped, "What do you mean you don't understand why I feel that way?" The first moment he challenged my psychological territory, I was furious at him, even though that was exactly what I was paying him to do, what I had invited him to do.

Because, as human beings, our anger center is firing

19

off all the time, and often very inappropriately, we must learn a whole complex set of ways of dealing with anger. Sometimes we have to think, as I had to do in relation to my analyst, "My anger is silly and immature. It's my fault." Or sometimes we have to conclude, "This person did impinge upon my territory, but it was an accident and there's no reason to get angry about it." Or, "Well, he did violate my territory a little bit, but it's no big deal. It's not worth blowing up about." But every once in a while, after we think about it for a couple of days, we may discern that someone really did seriously violate our territory. Then it may be necessary to go to that person and say, "Listen, I've got a real bone to pick with you." And sometimes it might even be necessary to get angry immediately and blast that person right on the spot.

So there are at least five different ways to respond when our anger center fires off. We not only need to know those ways of responding, but we also have to learn which response is appropriate in any given situation. It is an extraordinarily complex task, and it is therefore no wonder that very few people learn how to deal well with their anger before they are into their thirties or forties, and many never learn how to deal with it.

BLAME AND JUDGMENT

When we get angry and blame someone for making us angry, we are also making a judgment about that person—that he or she has sinned against us in some way.

Back when I was sixteen, I won my first and only speaking contest, on the topic "Judge not, and you will not be judged." Pontificating on Jesus' words, I said we shouldn't make any judgments of other people, and I won a can of tennis balls.

Today I no longer believe that it is possible to go through life without making judgments about other people. We have to make judgments about whom to marry or not marry, about when to intervene in the lives of our children or when not to intervene, whom to hire or whom to fire. Indeed, the quality of our life is determined precisely by the quality of our judgments.

I am not contradicting Jesus. First, His words are often misinterpreted. Jesus said, "Judge not, and you will not be judged"; He didn't say, "Never judge." But each time you judge, be prepared for judgment yourself. And second, He immediately went on to say, "Hypocrite! First take out the beam"—or two-by-four; he was a carpenter, remember—"out of your own eye, and then you will see clearly the mote"—or splinter—"in your brother's eye." In other words, Jesus said to judge yourself before you judge anyone else.

On this same subject Jesus also said, when confronting an angry crowd about to stone an adulterous woman, "Let that person who is without sin cast the first stone." Since all of us are sinners, does that mean we shouldn't cast any stones, that we shouldn't blame or judge anybody at all? In fact, no one threw a stone at the woman and Jesus then said to her: "Has no one condemned you? Then neither do I condemn you." Again he said to judge yourself before you judge others.

But despite the fact that we are all sinners, from time to time it is necessary that we cast a stone. It happens when we say to an employee, "This is the fourth year in a row that you have failed to meet your performance

21

objectives, this is the sixth time that I have caught you lying, and I'm afraid I'm going to let you go. I'm going to have to fire you.''

It is a terribly painful, brutal decision to fire someone. How do you know you are making the right judgment at the right time? How do you know you are right in blaming that person? The answer is, you don't. But you must always look at yourself first. Even though you might find that you have no choice but to fire that person, you may also find that there are many things you could have done—and did not do—that would have spared you that decision in the first place.

You need to ask yourself questions such as: ''Was I concerned about this person and his problems? Did I confront him when I caught him in the first instance of lying or was that confrontation too difficult for me and I let it slide until the situation got unbearable?'' If you answer such questions honestly, you may find that you will treat other employees differently, and you may be spared such a brutal judgment in the future.

THE AGONY OF NOT KNOWING

But how does one know exactly when the time has come for appropriate blame or judgment rather than self-criticism? When I first started public speaking, I didn't know whether it was the right thing to do. Was it really what God wanted me to do, or was I doing it out of an ego trip because I so enjoyed the roar of the crowd? I didn't know which and I agonized almost continually, looking for the answer. Finally, I got some help—and this reinforces my earlier point that everything that happens in life is there to aid our spiritual growth, and that we very much need each other in this regard. I had shared the agony I was going through with the person who sponsored my second speaking engagement. And about a month after that engagement, she sent me a poem she had written. She had not written it with me in mind, but the last lines of that poem were exactly what I needed to hear at the time:

The Truth is that I want It,
and the price I must pay
is to ask the question again and again and again.

Reading the poem, I realized that I had been looking for some kind of revelation—a formula—from God, which would say: "Yes, Scotty, go speak for all time." Or: "No, Scotty, don't ever open your mouth." But there was no formula, no easy answer, and I knew that what I was going to have to do each time I was invited to speak, each year that I renegotiated my lecture schedule, was to ask the question again and again and again: "Hey, God, is this what You want me to be doing now?" All any of us can do whenever confronted with a painful decision is to ask the question each time and once again agonize over the answer.

For example, if you are a mother or a father of a sixteen-year-old daughter who confronts you with a request to stay out until two a.m. on a particular Saturday night, what do you do? There are three ways that parents can respond. One is to say, "No, of course you can't. You know damn well your curfew is ten." Another way is to say, "Oh sure, dear, whatever you'd like." Those are what might be called right-wing and left-wing responses. But even though they are at opposite ends of the spectrum, there's something similar about them. They are shoot-from-the-hip, formulistic responses. They require no energy from the parents at all.

In my opinion what good parents would do is to ask themselves, "Should we or shouldn't we let her stay out until two a.m. this Saturday night?" And they will probably answer, "We don't know. It's true that her curfew is ten, but we set that when she was fourteen and there's probably no way that that's a realistic curfew anymore. On the other hand, at the party she's going to this Saturday night there's going to be alcohol and that's a little worrisome. But then, you know, she gets good grades in school, she does her homework, she's obviously got a sense of responsibility. Maybe we owe it to her to trust that sense of responsibility. On the other hand, the guy she's going out with looks to us like a total loser. Should we, or shouldn't we? Should we compromise? What's the right compromise? We don't know. Should it be midnight, should it be eleven, should it be one? We don't know."

Ultimately it does not matter so much what such parents decide. Because even though their daughter may not be terribly happy with the final decision, nonetheless she will know that she has been taken seriously, because her question has been taken seriously. And she will know that she is loved, because she is valuable enough for her parents to agonize over in their not knowing.

This is precisely why when I am asked, "Oh Dr. Peck, would you give me a formula so that I will know when it's the right time to blame and when it isn't the right time to blame?" I answer, "I cannot give you any such formula." Each instance is different, each is unique, and each time, if you are seeking the truth, you have to ask the question. Should you do this you will likely come to the correct decision, but you will also have to put up with the pain of not knowing for sure you have done the right thing.

TRUTH AND WILL

I have just spoken of both truth and God. Their proximity is no accident, because when we are talking about truth, we are talking about a something higher than ourselves. We are talking about searching for and submitting ourselves to a "Higher Power."

Lest you be tempted to dismiss that as a primitive "religious" notion, let me point out that science is truth-submitted behavior. The scientific method is nothing more than a series of conventions and procedures that we have developed over the centuries in the interest of truth, in order to combat our very human tendency to want to deceive ourselves. And so science is submitted to a higher arbiter, a higher power—truth.

Mahatma Gandhi said: "Truth is God and God is Truth." I believe that God is also light and love, but certainly truth. Thus I propose that the pursuit of scientific knowledge, even if it doesn't answer all questions, is, in its place, very godly behavior—behavior that involves submission to a higher power.

The single greatest cause of inappropriate blaming is the combination of a strong will with the lack of submission to a higher power. A strong will is, I believe, the best asset that a human being can possess, not because it guarantees success or goodness, but because a weak will pretty much guarantees failure. It is strong-willed people who do well in psychotherapy, who have that mysterious will to grow. And so it is a great asset and a great blessing. But all blessings are potential curses, all have their side effects. And the worst side effect of a strong will is a strong temper—anger.

The way I used to explain this to my patients was to tell them that having a weak will is like having a little donkey in your backyard. It can't hurt you very much; about the worst it can do is chomp on your tulips. But it can't help you that much either. Having a strong will, on the other hand, is like having a dozen Clydesdales in your backyard. Those horses are massive creatures and extremely strong, and if they are not properly trained, disciplined, and harnessed, they will knock your house down. On the other hand, if they are properly trained, disciplined, and harnessed, then with them you can literally move mountains.

But to what is the will to be harnessed? You cannot harness it to your own will because it thereby continues to remain unharnessed. Your will has to be harnessed to a power higher than yourself.

The distinction between the harnessed and the unharnessed will was beautifully drawn by Gerald May, in his book *Will and Spirit*, the first chapter of which is entitled "Willingness and Willfulness." Willfulness characterizes the unharnessed human will, whereas willingness identifies the strong will of a person who is willing to go where he or she is called or led by a higher power.

This distinction was also described poetically in that absolutely magnificent play *Equus*. The play is about a boy who has blinded six horses, and the psychiatrist treating him, Martin Dysart, who is going through a midlife spiritual crisis. At the end of the play, explaining how he has come through his crisis, Dysart says:

26

. . . I cannot call it ordained of God: I can't get that far. I will however pay it so much homage. There is now, in my mouth, this sharp chain. And it never comes out.

THE BLAMING GAME

It is no accident that people who commit the most evil in this world see no power higher than themselves. The evil are very strong-willed men and women. And because they are narcissistic, self-absorbed, and their will is supreme, they are the ones who are most into inappropriate and destructive blaming. They are the people who cannot—who will not—take the beam out of their own eye.

For most of us, if there is evidence around us that might point to our own sin and imperfection, if that evidence pushes us up against the wall, we usually come to recognize that something is wrong and we make some kind of self-correction. Those who do not I call "people of the lie" because one of their distinguishing characteristics is their ability to lie to themselves, as well as to others, and to insist on being ignorant of their own faults or wrongdoing. Their guiding motive is to feel good about themselves, at all costs, at all times, no matter what evidence there may be that points to their sin or imperfection. Rather than using it to make some kind of self-correction, they will instead—often at great expense of energy—set about trying to exterminate the evidence. They will use all the power at their disposal to impose their wills onto someone else in order to protect their own sick selves. And that is where most of their evil is committed, in that inappropriate extermination, that inappropriate blaming.

It is important to realize that blaming is fun. Anger is fun. Hatred is fun. And like any pleasurable activity, it is habit-forming—you get hooked on it.

Just how insidious this can be was brought home to me while reading some literature on demonic possession. I had come across several descriptions of the allegedly possessed person sitting in a corner, gnawing on his ankle. And this reminded me of some of the medieval paintings of Hell, in which you may see this same kind of figure—a damned person gnawing on his ankle. This seemed to be a very strange and very uncomfortable position to get oneself into. It didn't make sense to me until I read a little book by Frederick Buechner entitled *Wishful Thinking: A Theological ABC*. Right in the beginning of that book, under A, Buechner lists Anger and compares it to gnawing on a bone. There's always a little more tendon, always a little more marrow, always just a little bit left, and you keep gnawing on it. The only problem, Buechner says, is that the bone you're gnawing on is you.

Blaming others becomes a habit. And you end up gnawing on that bone, over and over and over again as you remind yourself how someone has wronged you. For this reason perhaps the most common of all psychological games might be called the Blaming Game. The term ''psychological game'' was coined by the late, great psychiatrist Eric Berne in his book *Games People Play*. Berne was not writing about playful games, although there can be some analogies, since psychological games certainly may be fun of a sort. Rather, he defined a psychological game as a ''repetitive interaction'' between two or more parties with an ''unspoken payoff.''

28

By repetitive interaction he meant something that is not only habituating but also stale, a kind of uncreative spinning of your wheels. By unspoken payoff he meant that there is something unsaid, something underneath the surface, underhanded, even something manipulative about psychological games.

The Blaming Game could also be called the "If It Weren't for You" Game. Most of us have played it. It is the most common of all marital games. For instance, Mary will say, "Well, I know I'm a nag, but that's because John has this emotional shell around him. I have to nag in order to get through to him. If it weren't for John's shell, I wouldn't be a nag." And John says, "Well, I know I have a shell around me, but that's because Mary's a nag. I have to have that shell in order to protect myself from her nagging. If it weren't for Mary's being a nag, I wouldn't have this shell."

So there is a kind of circular, repetitive quality to these games that is hard to interrupt. And in explaining how to stop a psychological game, Berne spoke one of the only two great truths I know that is not a paradox. He said that the only way to stop a game is to stop. That sounds simple, but in fact it is extremely difficult. Just how do you stop?

Remember what it's like to play Monopoly? You can be sitting there and saying, "You know, this is a really stupid game. We've been playing it for four hours now. It is really childish. I've got many better things I ought to be doing." But then you pass Go and say, "Give me my two hundred dollars."

No matter how much you might complain about it, as long as you keep collecting your two hundred dollars when you pass Go, the game goes on. And if it is a two-player game, it can go on forever unless one player gets up and says, "I'm not playing anymore."

The other player might then say, "But, Joe, you just passed Go. Here's your two hundred dollars."

"No, thanks, I'm not playing anymore."

"But, Joe, your two hundred dollars."

"Didn't you hear me? I'm not playing anymore."

The only way to stop a game is to stop.

Stopping the Blaming Game is called forgiveness. That is precisely what forgiveness is: the process of stopping, of ending, the Blaming Game. And it is tough.

THE REALITY OF EVIL

These days great numbers of people who are flocking to all types of New Age religions have somehow been seduced into believing that forgiveness is easy. Forgiveness is easy only when one becomes convinced that there really isn't such a thing as evil. And it just ain't so.

This misperception can lead people into certain traps, an example of which is found in a very popular New Age book called *Love Is Letting Go of Fear*, by Gerald Jampolsky, a fellow psychiatrist. His book is about forgiveness, a terribly important topic, but my problem with it is that Jampolsky makes it sound easy. He makes the blanket statement that rather than making judgments about people, we should look for the good within them, look for God within them, and affirm them.

I am always leery of blanket ideas and concepts, because they tend to be simplistic and get people into trouble. I am reminded of the words of an ancient Sufi master: "When I say weep, I do not mean for you to weep always. And when I say don't weep, I don't mean for you to become a permanent buffoon.'' But unfortunately, a great many people in the New Age movement have come to believe that "affirm" means "always affirm." I do agree that ninety percent of the time that is exactly what you should do, but maybe ten percent of the time—when you are confronted with someone like Hitler—affirming is precisely the worst thing that you could do.

Make no mistake, forgiveness and affirmation are not the same thing. Affirmation is a way to avoid looking at evil. It is saying, "Well, yes, my stepfather molested me as a child, but that was just his human failing, part of his being damaged in childhood." Forgiveness on the other hand requires facing evil squarely. It is saying to your stepfather: "What you did was wrong, despite your reasons for it. You committed a crime against me. And I know that, but I still forgive you."

That is not easy by any stretch of the imagination. Real forgiveness is a tough, tough process, but it is an absolutely necessary one for your mental health.

CHEAP FORGIVENESS

A great many people suffer from the problem I have come to call "cheap forgiveness." They come for their first session with a therapist and say, "Well, I know that I didn't have the greatest of childhoods, but my parents did the best they could and I've forgiven them." But as the therapist gets to know them, he finds that they have not forgiven their parents at all. They have simply convinced themselves that they have.

With such people, the first part of therapy consists of

putting their parents on trial. And it is a lot of work. It requires briefs for the prosecution, and briefs for the defense, and then appeals and counterappeals, until a judgment is finally brought in. Because this process requires so much work, most people opt for cheap forgiveness. But it is only when a guilty verdict is brought in—"No, my parents did not do the best they could; they could have done better; they committed certain offenses against me"—that the work of real forgiveness can begin.

You cannot pardon someone for a crime he hasn't committed. Only after a guilty verdict can there be a pardon.

BLAME AND MASOCHISM

Many people who come for therapy suffer from masochism. And by masochism I do not mean that they get their sexual jollies out of physical pain, but simply that in some strange way they are chronically self-destructive. A typical example would be that of a man who is brilliant and competent and who rises rapidly in his field but then, at the age of twenty-six when he's about to become the company's youngest vice president, he does something absolutely outrageous, blows it, and is fired. Because he's so bright, he is immediately hired by another firm, rises up meteorically, and at twenty-eight, just as he's about to be promoted, he again does something outrageous, blows it, and gets fired. And after this happens for the third time, he may come to realize that he's following some kind of chronically self-destructive pattern, a masochistic pattern.

Another example might be that of a woman who is

beautiful and brilliant and charming and competent, but who keeps dating one loser after another. People who exhibit such chronically self-destructive patterns are often also victims of cheap forgiveness. You'll find them saying, "Oh, I didn't have the greatest of childhoods, but my parents did the best they could."

To explain why cheap forgiveness just won't do, and why real forgiveness is essential to escape from such self-destructive traps, let me first explain something about what underlies this masochism. And the best way I know to do this is to look at psychodynamics in children, because what may be seen as psychopathology—mental illness—in adults is often perfectly normal in children. Let's take four-year-old Johnny, who wants to make mud pies in the living room. And Mommy says, "No, Johnny, you can't do it."

But Johnny insists, "Yes I can."

So Mommy insists, "No, you can't!"

And Johnny stomps up the stairs crying, goes into his bedroom, slams the door behind him, and begins to sob. After five minutes, the sobs die down, but he stays in his room, and after another half hour goes by, his mother thinks she should do something to cheer him up. She knows the one thing that Johnny loves more than anything else in the world is chocolate ice cream cones. So she very lovingly makes him a chocolate ice cream cone and goes upstairs, to find Johnny still sulking in a corner of his room.

"Here, Johnny, I made you a chocolate ice cream cone," she says. And Johnny yells "Neah!" and smacks it out of her hand.

That's masochism. Johnny is being given the one thing he loves more than anything else in the world and he's throwing it away. Why? Obviously, the reason is that, at that particular point in time, Johnny happens to be more into hating his mother than he is into loving ice cream. And that is what masochism is. It is always disguised sadism. Disguised hatred. Disguised rage.

The self-destructive people who come to therapy are playing the Blaming Game. They are saying at some unconscious level, "Look how my parents [because it is usually about their parents] screwed me up!" If that is the bone they are gnawing on—and remember, they are always gnawing on themselves —it is their primary unconscious motive to show the world how those bastards screwed them up. If they are healthy and doing pretty well financially, if their marriages are working and their children are turning out golden, how can they say, "Look how they screwed me up!" They can't, can they? But, if that is their bone, the only way they can keep gnawing on it is by staying screwed up. And the only way they can change that is to forgive, truly forgive, their parents, and that is tough, tough work.

THE NECESSITY OF FORGIVENESS

One patient of mine, whose parents had put him through hell as a child and who was working through this, said to me: "You know, I could forgive them if I could go to them and tell them the ways they've hurt me and they would apologize. Or even if they would just listen. But if I did go and tell them how they'd hurt me, they'd say I was just making these things up. They'd refuse to even remember what they have done. I'm the one who has had all of the pain. They gave me all the pain. They haven't had any of it, but you're expecting *me* to forgive *them*?"

And I said, "Yes."

The reason is that it is necessary for healing. Painful though it is, I must explain to such patients that they are going to stay screwed up until they can forgive their parents, whether or not their parents apologize or even listen.

There are a couple of standard things that I used to hear from patients who were resisting the necessity of real forgiveness. A patient would ask me, "Why do we have to talk about all this bad stuff? We're always talking about all the bad things my parents did, and that's really unfair to them. You know, they did some good things, too. This is unbalanced."

And I would say, "Obviously your parents did some good things. For one thing, you're alive, and you wouldn't even be alive unless they did something right. But the reason that we focus on the bad stuff is because of Sutton's law."

My patient would then look blankly at me. "Sutton's law?

And I would say, "Yes, it's a law named after Willie Sutton, who was a famous bank robber. When Sutton was asked by a reporter why he robbed banks, he said, 'Because that's where the money is.' "

We psychotherapists focus on the bad stuff because that's where the payoff is—not only for us but for our patients—because that's where the wounds and scars are, because those are the areas that need healing.

Another even more primitive thing I used to hear people say when they first came into therapy was, "Why do we have to dredge up all this stuff from the past? Why not just forget it?"

The reason is that we cannot forget anything. We cannot truly forget. We can only truly forgive, although in order to avoid doing the hard work of forgiveness we often try to push the offense out of our minds.

With the caveat that sometimes people may invent false memories, through the psychological mechanism known as repression, it is possible to push a memory of something that happened to us out of consciousness. We cannot consciously remember it, but it doesn't go away when we do this. In fact, it becomes a ghost that haunts us and makes things worse than if we remembered it.

It is possible, for instance, for women who have been repeatedly sexually molested—week after week after week for a period of two or three years by their fathers or stepfathers—to actually forget that. They can't even remember that it ever happened, because they have repressed it. But then these women end up in therapy, usually because the relationships they are trying to form with the men in their lives are abominable. That early experience, which they cannot remember, continues to haunt them.

And so I would tell my patients that we cannot really forget about anything. The best we can do is to come to terms with it, to such a degree that we can remember it without pain. Therefore, the first step in the safety of the therapeutic alliance is to remember the crimes that were committed. Then comes the anger. It must come, as must the trial and the naming of the crimes. But beyond a certain point, the longer you hold on to that anger, the longer you will continue to hurt yourself.

The process of forgiveness—indeed, the chief reason for forgiveness—is selfish. The reason to forgive others is *not* for their sake. They are not likely to know that they need to be forgiven. They're not likely to remember their offense. They are likely to say, "You just made it up." They may even be dead. The reason to forgive is for our own sake. For our own health. Because beyond that point needed for healing, if we hold on to our anger, we stop growing and our souls begin to shrivel.

CHAPTER THREE

The Issue of Death and Meaning

There is a poem entitled "Limited" by Carl Sandburg:

> I am riding on a limited express, one of the crack trains of the nation.
> Hurtling across the prairie into blue haze and dark air go fifteen all-steel coaches holding a thousand people.
> (All the coaches shall be scrap and rust and all the men and women laughing in the diners and sleepers shall pass to ashes.)
> I ask a man in the smoker where he is going and he answers: "Omaha."

This is—in case you haven't guessed it—a poem about death, a particularly succinct and incisive summary of our attitude toward this largely ignored subject, but one which I have been fascinated with for as long as I can remember. You could say I've had a romance with death since I was a teenager, which is not to imply that I've been suicidal. It was, rather, a reaction to the environment I was raised in. My boyhood home was a place where superficialities were considered to be of the utmost importance. It was crucial in one's life to know which fork to use.

Some years ago there was a fad—preppie presents for Christmas. I bought one for my wife, an apron with a big mallard duck on it and above that, printed in big letters: BEFORE TRUTH THE RIGHT FORK. That is what my childhood was like. "Clothes maketh the man," my parents intoned on dozens of occasions. Disillusionment was bound to follow, because sooner or later it was inevitable that I would run across a well-dressed idiot.

So, at a relatively early age, perhaps out of a spirit of rebellion, I said to myself: "Forget the superficialities. What is it that's *really* important?" I began to develop a habit of looking beneath the surface of things, a habit that has stood me in good stead ever since. And when I asked what is most important about our human existence, the first answer that came to my mind was that it is limited. We are all going to die. That's when my romance with death began.

As an adult I've come to recognize that death may not be *the* most important thing about our existence, but it is perhaps the second most important thing. And part of growing up is recognizing the fact that we are all going to die. We are all going to turn to scrap and rust and ashes.

The knowledge that life is limited fills many of us with a sense of meaninglessness. Since we're going to be chopped down by the Grim Reaper like so much straw, what possible meaning could there be to our paltry human existence? Granted, we might live on for a while through our children, but as the generations pass in relatively short order, the memory of our very name will be lost.

You may recall the famous poem by Shelley, "Ozymandias," in which he describes the remains of a statue standing in the desert. On the pedestal is inscribed:

"My name is Ozymandias, King of Kings:
Look on my works, ye Mighty, and despair!"

Yet all that is left of the statue is the pedestal, two vast and trunkless legs of stone, and a shattered visage half buried in the sand—and no one can remember who the man was.

So even if you are among the very few who manage to leave their imprint upon human history, as the centuries roll on, even that imprint will be lost.

"Life's but a walking shadow," laments Shakespeare's Macbeth. "It is a tale told by an idiot, full of sound and fury, signifying nothing."

THE FEAR OF DEATH

Can that be right? That life signifies nothing—and even if it does, death wipes its meaning away? Is it all for naught?

I do not believe so. Death is the opposite of what we think. Death is not a taker-away but rather a giver of meaning.

More than anything else, my romance with death has given me a sense of the meaningfulness of this life. Death is a magnificent lover. If you are suffering from a sense of meaninglessness or ennui, there is nothing better I can suggest to you than that you strike up a serious relationship with the end of your existence. Like any great love, death is full of mystery and that's where much of the excitement comes from. Because as you struggle with the mystery of your death, you will discover the meaning of your life.

Of course, most people have very little taste for struggling with the idea of their death. They do not even want to think about it. They want to exclude it from their awareness, thereby limiting their consciousness. Thus, the title of Sandburg's poem, "Limited," not only refers to the train but carries a larger meaning. Life is limited and the man who says he is going to Omaha is limited in his awareness of his true destination: death.

But you will find that people who are not so limited—like many of the great writers and thinkers—sooner or later become fascinated with death. Albert Schweitzer wrote:

We must all become familiar with the thought of death if we want to grow into really good people. We need not think of it every day or every hour. But when the path of life leads us to some vantage point where the scene around us fades away and we contemplate the distant view right to the end, let us not close our eyes. Let us pause for a moment, look at the distant view, and then carry on. Thinking about death in this way produces love for life. When we are familiar with death we accept each week, each day, as a gift. Only if we are able thus to accept life—bit by bit—does it become precious.

That is not the usual view of death. In my practice of psychotherapy, I found that I had to push at least half of my patients to face the reality of their death. Indeed, their reluctance to do so seemed to be a part of their

41

illness. They simultaneously found their life tedious and frightening. They failed to visit friends in the hospital, skipped over the obituary pages, forgot to write condolence letters. And at night they would wake up drenched in sweat, dreaming of drowning. Unless I could get them to break through these self-imposed limits to their consciousness, there could be no full healing. We cannot live with courage and confidence until we can have a relationship with our own death. Indeed, we cannot live fully unless there is something that we are willing to die for.

These limits on people's consciousness can sometimes be debilitating. Early in my practice, I was visited by a man who arrived in a state of panic some three days after his brother-in-law had committed suicide by shooting himself in the head with a pistol. This man was so terrified he couldn't even come to my office alone. He had to come with his wife holding his hand. He sat down and began rambling: "You know, my brother-in-law, he shot himself in the head. I mean he had this pistol, and I mean all it took was just this, I mean just an ounce of pressure and he's dead now. I mean that was all it took. And if I had a gun, I mean I don't have a gun, but if I had a gun and I wanted to kill myself, I mean all it would take would just be—I mean I don't want to kill myself, but I mean—all it—just this much."

As I listened to him, it was clear that what had precipitated his panic was not grief over his brother-in-law's death, but rather that this event had put him in touch with his own mortality, and I told him so.

He instantly contradicted me. "Oh, I'm not afraid of dying!"

That's when his wife broke in, and she said, "Well,

42

dear, maybe you ought to tell the doctor about the hearses and the funeral parlors."

He then proceeded to explain to me that he had a phobia about hearses and funeral parlors—indeed, to such a degree that every day walking to and from work, he would go three blocks out of his way—six blocks each day—just to avoid passing a funeral parlor. Also, whenever a hearse drove by, he had to turn away, or better yet, duck into a doorway, or even better, into a store.

"You really do have quite a fear of death," I said. But he continued to insist, "No, no, no, I'm not afraid of dying. It's just those damn hearses and funeral parlors that bother me."

Psychodynamically, phobias usually result from a mechanism called displacement. This man was so afraid of dying that he couldn't even face up to his fear of dying and displaced it onto funeral parlors and hearses.

Because I often use psychiatric patients as my examples, you may think they are more cowardly and frightened than most. Not so. Those who come to psychotherapy are the wisest and most courageous among us. Everyone has problems, but what they often do is to try to pretend that those problems don't exist, or they run away from those problems, or drink them down, or ignore them in some other way. It's only the wiser and braver among us who are willing to submit themselves to the difficult process of self-examination that happens in a psychotherapist's office.

The fact of the matter is that we live in a cowardly, death-denying culture. A psychiatrist colleague told me once that in her town, after one high school student died of leukemia and another died in an automobile crash, the juniors and seniors petitioned the principal to introduce an elective, noncredit course on death and dying. A minister even stepped forward and offered to organize the course and find the teachers for it for free, so it wouldn't cost anyone anything.

But any new course in that school system had to be approved by the school board, which immediately voted nine to one against it on the grounds that it was morbid. About thirty or forty people wrote letters to the newspaper protesting that decision, and one of the editors of the paper wrote an editorial on the subject. There was a sufficient hue and cry to force the school board to reconsider its decision. The board did that and once again voted nine to one against the course.

It was not coincidental, in my view, that, as my colleague recounted, everyone who wrote a letter to the newspaper, the editor who wrote the editorial, and the one member of the school board who voted for the course were all people who either were in therapy or had been in therapy. As I said, psychiatric patients are not more cowardly than most. They are more courageous.

CHOOSING WHEN TO DIE

In our death-denying culture, death is viewed as an accident, as something that strikes us down without any rhyme or reason, and without our having any kind of control over it whatsoever. It's a sad state of affairs because we are caught in a kind of vicious cycle. Because we are so afraid of death, we are afraid to get close enough to it to see that we have less to fear than we thought.

Our cultural vision of death as an accident without rhyme or reason is just plain wrong. Most of us will, in fact, *choose* when, where, or how we die. It may seem shocking, but it is true. Most of us—on some level, in some way—will make that choice. I am not talking about suicides or one-car accidents or other incidents that might be suicides. I am not talking about alcoholics who drink themselves to death, or emphysemics who continue to smoke. Nor am I even talking about any of the well-known psychosomatic disorders. I am talking about medical disorders like heart disease and cancer, and there is scientific evidence to support my contention.

About thirty years ago when open-heart surgery first began—and was much more dangerous than it is now—everyone got into the act. And it was discovered that the people who could best predict how someone would do as an open-heart surgery patient were not the heart surgeons, not the cardiologists, but the psychiatrists. In one such study psychiatrists interviewed patients prior to their surgeries and, based on their answers, divided them into high-, medium-, and low-risk groups. In the low-risk group they found the kind of man who, when asked to talk about his heart surgery, would say: "Well, you know, it's scheduled for Friday and I'm really scared out of my wits about it. But for the past eight years, I haven't been able to do anything. I haven't been able to play golf, I've been so short of breath, and my surgeon tells me that if I survive the surgery and the postoperative period, I'll be as good as new in six weeks and be able to play golf six weeks from Friday. Hey, that's the first of September. I've got my tee time all arranged, and I'm going to be out there at eight o'clock in the morning and the dew is going to be still on the grass. I've got every hole mapped out in my mind."

Now, in the high-risk group there might be a woman who, when asked to talk about her surgery, would say:

"Well, what about it?" And the psychiatrist would prompt: "Why are you having it, why do you need it?" And she would respond: "My doctor told me to."

"Are you looking forward to what you'll be able to do after your surgery?"

"I haven't thought about it."

"You've been so short of breath you haven't been able to go shopping for the past eight years. Aren't you looking forward to going shopping again?"

"Oh good gracious no. I'd be too afraid to drive after all these years."

Taking just the extremes, what this study found—if my memory serves me correctly—was that forty percent of the patients in the high-risk group died, and two percent of the people in the low-risk group died. Same heart disease, same heart surgeons, same heart surgery, and yet a twentyfold difference in mortality rate, which could be predicted before the surgery.

Another study with startling results was conducted by David Siegel, a psychiatrist at Stanford University, who studied two groups of women with metastatic cancer. The first group was given standard medical care; the second group also received standard medical care, but in addition was required to undergo psychotherapy. Not surprisingly, the second group complained of less anxiety, less depression, and less pain. But the astounding thing is that after all but three of the women in the study died, Siegel realized that those in therapy had lived twice as long as those in the other group.

"MIRACLE" CURES

Doctors have known for centuries that there are occasional, very rare cases of what are known as spontaneous remissions of cancer. You've heard of instances where doctors operate on a person and say, "We opened him up and he was just riddled with cancer and there was nothing we could do. The cancer was inoperable. All we could do was close him up. At most he's got six months to live." But then five, ten years later, that person is still alive without a trace of cancer.

You might think that physicians would be absolutely fascinated by such rare cases, and would have thoroughly studied and investigated them. They haven't. For years doctors have insisted that such a thing was impossible, and it is only in the last fifteen years that studies have been instituted. It is still too early for all the results to be statistically significant—that is, totally up to scientific standards—but there are indications that one of the similarities in all those rare cases is a tendency on the part of the patients to make very profound changes in their lives. Once told they have a year to live, they seem to say to themselves, "I'm darned if I want to live out my days still working for IBM. What I want to do is refinish furniture. That's what I've always wanted to do." Or, "If I've only got a year to live, I'm darned if I want to live it with this fuddy-duddy old husband of mine." So after they make such decisions and such changes in their lives, their cancer goes away.

This phenomenon intrigued some researchers at UCLA, who decided to see if maybe a life change could be induced via therapy. But their problem was finding patients who were willing to try it. Typically, a psychiatrist would go to someone who had been diagnosed as having inoperable cancer and say, "We have some reason to believe that if you're willing to enter psychother-

47

apy and look at your life and make some significant changes, you could prolong your life.''

And initially the patient seemed overjoyed. ''Oh, doctor, doctor, you're the first person that's given me any hope!''

So the psychiatrist says, ''A group of patients like you are meeting with us in room four tomorrow morning at ten. Would you like to come and talk about this?''

''Oh yes, doctor, I'll be there.''

But come ten o'clock the next morning, the patient doesn't show up. So the psychiatrist inquires and the patient says, ''I'm sorry, it just sort of slipped my mind.''

''Are you still interested?''

''Oh yes, doctor.''

''We're having another meeting down in room four at three o'clock tomorrow afternoon. Are you free then?''

''Oh yes, I'll be there.''

Again the patient doesn't show up. So the psychiatrist tries one more time and finally says, ''Perhaps you're not really so keen on this idea of psychotherapy.''

And the patient finally admits it. ''You know, doc, I have been thinking about it, and I really am too old a dog to learn new tricks.''

This isn't necessarily to be condemned. We do become old dogs, and are sometimes too tired to learn new tricks. Doctors are equally guilty of this. I constantly run into extremely well educated physicians who seem to believe that disease has to have only one cause—psychological or physical. It is beyond their comprehension to imagine that a disease, like the trunk of a tree, could have two roots simultaneously, or even more.

48

The reality is that virtually all diseases are psycho-spiritual-socio-somatic. There are exceptions, of course, like congenital disorders or cerebral palsy, for example. But even in such cases, the *will* to live can significantly prolong life and enhance its quality.

Unfortunately, the reverse is also true. When I was stationed with the armed services on Okinawa, I was asked to treat a nineteen-year-old woman suffering from hyperemesis gravidarum—excessive vomiting in pregnancy. I learned that she had grown up on the East Coast and had a pathological attachment to her mother. At the age of seventeen she had been sent to live with an uncle on the West Coast, and she had started to vomit. She was not pregnant then. She vomited so much that she had to be sent back East, where she remained very happy and healthy until she got pregnant by a soldier who married her and brought her to Okinawa. No sooner had she set foot off the airplane than she started to vomit, and within a very few days she was in the hospital.

I had the right, if my patients were sufficiently ill, to medevac them back home. And I knew that if I sent this patient home, her vomiting would stop immediately. I also knew that it would probably hopelessly entrench this pathology of vomiting every time she was separated from her mother.

In my omnipotence back then, I decided I would not send her home. I told her, ''You've got to grow up and learn how to live separate from your mother.'' And she got better enough to be discharged from the hospital. But then she got worse and came back in. She was vomiting again, and I told her again that I was not going to send her home. Again she got better enough to be discharged. Two days later in her apartment, however, she suddenly

49

dropped dead. She was nineteen years old and four months pregnant. They did an autopsy and never found out why she died. I deeply regretted my own decision, of course. But it is my belief that, for whatever reason, sometime in her life she had made a decision to be a child. I wouldn't let her be a child, so, rather than assume responsibility, she died.

SOMATIC AND PSYCHOSOMATIC DISORDERS

When I was in medical school, we referred to conditions like schizophrenia, manic-depressive disease, and alcoholism as "functional" disorders. By that word "functional" we hedged our bet and acknowledged that maybe one day researchers would discover some very subtle neuroanatomic defect or some kind of biological problem. But we really believed that these disorders were all psychological. And as psychiatrists we had the psychology of them all mapped out.

In the last thirty years, however, we have learned that there are profound biological roots to all of these psychiatric disorders, and more. In fact, one of the problems that we're facing today is that psychiatrists have become so enamored of biochemistry that we're in danger of forgetting all of the old psychological wisdom, some of which is still very true. Conditions like schizophrenia are not *just* somatic disorders. They are also psycho-spiritual-socio-somatic disorders. And the same applies to diseases like cancer. All have multifaceted causes—somatic and psychosomatic.

The psychosomatic component to our suffering has been recognized in our language for centuries. There's something that psychiatrists refer to as "organ language," which reflects a kind of psychosomatic wisdom. For example: "He gives me a pain in the neck," or, "I've got butterflies in my stomach," or, "My heart is breaking." Any number of people go to emergency rooms late at night with chest pain—with or without heart attacks—just after they have undergone some kind of heartbreak.

Disorders of the spine are disorders of courage. And again, this is reflected in our language. We say, "He's got a yellow streak up his spine," or, "He's spineless," or, "Boy, she's really got backbone," or, "She's got lots of spine." I have suffered from back problems for most of my life, specifically a condition called spondylosis, which has been particularly severe in my neck. To look at an X ray of my neck, you would think I was two hundred years old. When I was first diagnosed with this condition, I asked neurosurgeons and orthopedic surgeons, "What causes my neck to look so old?" And they would say, "Well, probably when you were a kid you broke your neck."

I have never broken my neck. But when I told them that, all they could say was, "In that case we really don't know what caused your spondylosis." I was very glad of that answer, because few doctors are willing to go so far as to say, "I don't know. "

Actually, I do know a good deal about what caused my spondylosis. I found out some thirteen years ago when, because my condition was driving me crazy with pain as well as paralyzing one of my arms, I underwent lengthy and serious neurosurgery. I said to myself at that time, "Scotty, you know, if you don't want to undergo this very expensive, life-threatening surgery every couple of years—and eventually, to take care of the problem they're going to have to cut off your neck—maybe you might look at whether there's any role you are playing in this disorder. Is there any way that you are feeding into this?''

As soon as I was willing to ask that question, I immediately realized there was. I realized that for most of my life I'd been walking on the cutting edge of my profession, and I'd always been fearful of generating hostility. I had run into some hostility, although never as much as I anticipated, so my fear had a basis. But I had been going through life with my head and neck hunched down like a football player about ready to buck into the defensive line of the Pittsburgh Steelers. Try holding your head and neck that way for thirty years, and you too will know something about what causes spondylosis.

Of course, nothing is simple. There are multiple causes for most diseases. Although not to the same degree as I have, it so happens that my father, my mother, and my brother have suffered from an unusual amount of neck spondylosis, even though they were never renowned for ''sticking their necks out.'' So there's obviously a biological—genetic or hereditary—component to my condition. Remember my contention that virtually all disorders are not only psychosomatic but psycho-spiritual-socio-somatic.

I'm not breaking new ground here. Much has been written about the relationship between body and mind. So many are becoming aware of the psychosomatic component of disease that some people these days feel guilty when they get sick. It is, of course, unnecessary to go around feeling guilty every time you get a cold or the flu. But it does behoove you, if you have a serious or a chronic illness, to take a look at yourself and ask whether you may be playing some role in your illness.

But if you do so, for God's sake, be gentle with yourself. Life in some ways is *meant* to be stressful, and it wears us down. Please remember that sooner or later we all have to die from one damn psychosomatic disorder or another.

Again, I do not mean to imply that all terminal cancer is psychosomatic and that a children's cancer ward—with a four-year-old dying from an adrenal carcinoma and a six-year-old dying from a medulloblastoma and an eight-year-old dying from a Wilms' tumor—is nothing more than a repository for childhood suicides. I do not mean to imply that the victims of an airplane crash deliberately came together at the airport in a mass suicide attempt. Or that six million Jews willingly went to their deaths during the Holocaust. But when we consider death simply as an accident, we are ignoring not only the reality of most death but also its mystery.

UNDERSTANDING DEATH

One of the landmarks in our growing awareness of the true nature of death was the publication of the book *On Death and Dying* by Elisabeth Kubler-Ross, M.D. Until that time, death was the sole province of the priest. Doctors were interested in life, and life was for the living. Death was left to the morticians. But Kubler-Ross actually dared to talk to people who were dying, and dared to ask them what they were thinking of, what they were feeling about their impending deaths. She created a veritable revolution. A scant decade later there were courses on death and dying across the country. And the hospice, a place where people could go to die—a whole new institution—was invented or reinvented. It was as if she had caused a dam to burst.

Her work led to other books on the subject, among them *Life after Life* by Raymond Moody and *At the Hour of Death* by Karlis Osis and Erlendur Haraldsson, who wrote of the moment of death and near-death experiences. There is a startling unanimity about what they've found. Raymond Moody, a scientist and a psychiatrist, reported that most of the people who remember their near-death experience relate a variation on the following sequence. First, they remember looking, as if from the ceiling, at their own bodies lying on a bed, and seeing very exactly what the nurses and doctors are doing to them. The next thing that happens—the only frightening part of the experience—involves going through a dark tunnel of some kind. They are whisked through rapidly, and when they come out of the tunnel, they are confronted by a light, which is perceived as God or sometimes as Jesus. And this being of light requires that they review their lives. In doing so, they tend to realize what a mess their lives were, but the being is extraordinarily loving and forgiving. Then the being directs them to go back, which they do reluctantly but in obedience to the light.

Often people who have had such experiences, according to Moody, were not previously spiritual, but became so afterwards. And invariably they have come to believe in life after death and have a much diminished fear of dying.

Isn't it interesting that when we get up close enough to death, we see that we've got much less to fear from it than we thought? But that might not bring you comfort.

You might be saying, "What does it have to do with this life? What possible meaning could there be to this temporary existence of ours?"

If you ask such questions, I suspect it's precisely because you are well aware that your existence is limited, and you are looking for its meaning. But suppose the search for meaning is itself meaningful. Suppose that is part of the game, part of why we're here. Could we be here to search for something? If the answer is yes, then death impels that search.

As I have struggled with the mystery of my death, seeking the meaning of this life, I have found what I am looking for. It is very simple. *We are here to learn.* Everything that happens to us helps our learning. And nothing helps us to learn more than death.

I have also come to conclude that we have been given an ideal learning environment. I defy you, in your imagination, to come up with a more ideal environment for human learning than life, than this life. It seems to me, in my gloomier moments, a kind of celestial boot camp, replete with obstacle courses which have been, almost fiendishly, designed for our learning. And I think the most fiendishly designed of all obstacles in life is the obstacle of sex. In actuality, death is a consequence of our sexuality.

Organisms at the bottom of the evolutionary scale do not reproduce sexually. They simply clone. They bud, and their genetic material goes on and on and on. They literally never die, unless somebody happens to come along and squish them. They experience no such thing as aging or natural death. Only when you get high enough in the evolutionary scale do you find sexual reproduction, and the moment you do, you find the phenomenon

55

of aging and natural death. There's a price to everything.

We learn best when we have a deadline. What a wonderful word! In my practice of psychotherapy, I often employed a particularly potent and useful technique working with groups. When the members of a group seemed to be acting as if they had all the time in the world, I would come in one day and say, "Okay, guys, this group has only got six months more to live. I'm ending this group in six months. You've had it in six months." It was amazing how quickly people who had been sitting around on their duffs doing absolutely nothing could move once they were given a deadline.

In individual therapy as well, a deadline can be equally potent. The termination of a beloved relationship between a patient and a therapist can sometimes be used to symbolize the whole issue of death and give the patient an opportunity—that most people would never otherwise encounter—to work through death.

STAGES OF DEATH AND GROWTH

Elisabeth Kubler-Ross found that people who were dying went through certain stages—and they occur in this order:

- denial
- anger
- bargaining
- depression
- acceptance

The first stage is denial. They deny. They say, "The

lab must have gotten my tests mixed up with somebody else's. It can't be me, it can't be happening to me.'' But that doesn't work for very long. So they get angry. They get angry at the doctors, angry at the nurses, angry at the hospital, angry at their relatives, angry at God.

When anger doesn't get them anywhere, then they start to bargain. They say, "Maybe if I go back to church and start praying again, my cancer will go away.'' Or, ''Maybe if I start being nicer to my children for a change, my kidneys will improve.'' And when that doesn't get results, they begin to realize the jig is up, and they're really going to die. At that point, they become depressed.

If they can hang in there and do what we therapists call ''the work of depression,'' then they can emerge at the other end of their depression and enter the fifth stage, of acceptance. This is a stage of great spiritual calm and tranquillity, and even light. People who have accepted death have a light in them. It's almost as if they had already died and were resurrected in some psychospiritual sense. It's a beautiful thing to see.

It is, however, not very common. Most people do not die in this beautiful fifth stage of acceptance. They die still denying, still angry, still bargaining, or still depressed. The reason is that the work of depression is so painful and difficult that when they hit it they usually retreat back into denial or anger or bargaining.

Although Kubler-Ross didn't recognize it at the time, the most fascinating thing about this is that we go through exactly the same stages in exactly the same order any time we make any significant step in our psychological or spiritual growth. Any time we make any giant step forward through the desert, any time we

57

make any significant improvement in ourselves, we go through this process of denial, anger, bargaining, depression, and acceptance.

Let's imagine, for example, that there is a serious flaw in my personality, and that my friends start criticizing me for the manifestations of this flaw. What's my first reaction? I say, "She must have just gotten out of the wrong side of bed this morning." Or, "He must really be angry at his wife. Doesn't have anything to do with me." Denial.

If they keep on criticizing me, then I say: "What gives them the right to stick their noses in my business? They don't know what it's like to be in my shoes. Why don't they mind their own damn business!" I may even tell them that. Anger.

But if they love me enough to keep on criticizing me, then I begin to think: "Gee, I really haven't told them lately what a good job they're doing." And I go around giving them lots of pats on the back, smiling at them a lot, hoping that this will shut them up. Bargaining.

But if they truly do love me enough to keep on criticizing, then maybe I get to the point where I think, "Could they be right? Could there possibly be something wrong with the great Scott Peck?" And if I answer yes, then that's depressing. But if I can hang in there with that depressing notion—that maybe there really is something wrong with me—and start to wonder what it might be, if I contemplate it and analyze it and isolate it, and identify it, then I can go about the process of killing it and purifying myself of it. Having done—fully completed—the *work* of depression, I will then emerge at the other end as a new man, a resurrected human being, a better person.

LEARNING TO DIE

None of this is really new. In *The Road Less Traveled* I quoted Seneca as saying, almost two thousand years ago, "Throughout the whole of life, one must continue to learn how to live, and what will amaze you even more, throughout life one must learn to die." Learning how to live and learning how to die go together. In order to learn how to live, we have to come to terms with our death, because our death reminds us of the limit of our existence. Thus we become conscious of the brevity of our time in order to make full use of our time.

Don Juan, the old Mexican Indian guru in the books by Carlos Castaneda, referred to death as an ally. In Don Juan's parlance, allies were fearsome powers that had to be wrestled with before they could be tamed. And so it is with death. We have to wrestle with it, struggle with the mystery of death, before we can tame it sufficiently to put it on our left shoulder, as Don Juan did. And sitting there, we can continually, day in and day out, benefit from its wise counsel.

"Ally" signifies a friend, but, at least in the Western cultures, we are not accustomed to looking at death as a friend. In the Eastern cultures, in Hindu and Buddhist religions, death is supposedly more welcome than in ours. Indeed, in reincarnation theory—to which both those religions subscribe —the whole reward, the whole goal is death. The idea is that we keep being recycled—reborn and reborn and reborn—until we have learned what it is we are on earth to learn. Then and only then can we get off the wheel of rebirth and finally die for good.

Whether you subscribe to it or not, note that in reincarnation theory the purpose of life is also to learn. Actually, there is no evidence that Hindus or Buddhists are any less afraid of death than the rest of us. It is normal to be afraid of dying. Dying is a going into the unknown, and to a degree it is very healthy to be fearful of entering the unknown. What is not healthy is to try to ignore it.

One of the most frequent criticisms I hear from my atheist friends is that religion is a crutch for old people as they face the mystery, the terror of their death. I think they are correct that a mature religion begins in a struggle with the mystery of death. But I think they are incorrect that it is a crutch, as if it would somehow be braver to face a godless existence without afterlife and without meaning. I think that by acknowledging and facing up to the importance of death, the people who become religious may actually be the more courageous. Atheists, in my opinion, tend to deny the importance of death, proclaiming it to be nothing more than a cessation of the heartbeat, and immediately turn away. It is a kind of avoidance. They do not want to get close enough to death to look beneath the surface.

Mind you, the majority of churchgoers do not have any more taste for struggling with the mystery of their death than do atheists. Most churchgoers practice superficial, inherited, hand-me-down kinds of religion, which—like hand-me-down clothes—may keep them warm but are still just trappings. This is the reason for the saying ''God has no grandchildren.'' We cannot relate to God through our parents. We have to establish a direct relationship with God. We cannot let someone else—our ministers, our leaders, or our parents—struggle with the mystery of our death. There are certain parts of the spiritual journey through life which must be done in solitude, and one of those is struggling with the mystery of death. You cannot let anyone else take up that struggle for you.

So, many churchgoers avoid the issue of death like the plague. Most Christian denominations have even taken Jesus off the cross. If you ask them why, they say that they want to emphasize the Resurrection over the Crucifixion. But sometimes I can't help but wonder if they simply don't want to see all that blood and gore and the reality of that death in front of them to remind them of their own.

FEAR OF DEATH AND NARCISSISM

But why are we are so often excessively afraid of death?

It is primarily because of our narcissism. Narcissism is an extraordinary, complex phenomenon. Some of it is necessary as the psychological side of our survival instinct, but most of it past childhood is self-destructive. Unbridled narcissism is the principal precursor of psychospiritual illness. The healthy spiritual life consists in a progressive growing out of narcissism. And while the failure to grow out of it is extremely common, it is also extremely destructive.

When psychiatrists talk about injuries to pride, we call them narcissistic injuries. And on any scale of narcissistic injuries, death is the ultimate. We suffer little narcissistic injuries all the time: a classmate calls us stupid, for example; we're the last to be chosen for someone's volleyball team; colleges turn us down; employers criticize us; we get fired; our children reject us. As a result of these narcissistic injuries, either we become embittered or we grow. But death is the big one. Nothing threatens our narcissistic attachment to ourselves and our self-conceit more than our impending obliteration. So it is utterly natural that we should fear death.

There are two ways to deal with that fear: the common way and the smart way. The common way is to put it out of our mind, limit our awareness of it, try not to think about it. That tends to work fine when we're young. But the longer we put it off, the closer it gets. And after a while everything begins to become a reminder of death—the graduation of a child, the illness of a friend, the creak in a joint. In other words, the common way is not very smart. In fact, the more we put off facing our death, the more frightening our old age is going to be.

The smart way is to face death as early as possible. And in doing so, we can realize something really rather simple. And that is, insofar as we can overcome our narcissism—and we can probably never do this totally— we can overcome our fear of death.

For people who succeed at this, the prospect of death becomes a magnificent stimulus for their psychological and spiritual growth. "Since I'm going to die anyway," they think, "what's the point of preserving this attachment I have to my silly old self?" And so they set forth on a journey toward selflessness.

It is not an easy journey. The tentacles of our narcissism are subtle and penetrating and have to be hacked away day after day, week after week, month after month, year after year, decade after decade.

Forty years after first recognizing my own narcissism, I am still hacking away.

It is not an easy journey, but what a worthwhile journey it is. Because the further we proceed in diminishing our narcissism, our self-centeredness and sense of self-importance, the more we discover ourselves becoming not only less fearful of death, but also less fearful of life. And we become more loving. No longer burdened by the need to protect ourselves, we are able to lift our eyes off ourselves and to truly recognize others. And we begin to experience a sustained, underlying kind of happiness that we've never experienced before as we become progressively more self-forgetful and hence more able to remember God.

This is the central message of all the great religions: Learn how to die. Again and again they tell us that the path away from narcissism is the path toward meaning. Buddhists and Hindus speak of this in terms of the necessity for self-detachment, and, indeed, for them even the notion of the self is an illusion. Jesus spoke of it in similar terms: ''Whosoever will save his life [that is, whosoever will hold on to his narcissism] will lose it. And whosoever will lose his life for my sake will find it.''

CHAPTER FOUR

The Taste for Mystery

For many years now I have had a mentor. I have never met him, because he comes to me from a sweet little Hasidic story. He was a rabbi who lived in a small Russian town at the turn of the century. And after twenty years of pondering the very deepest religious questions and spiritual issues in life, he finally came to the conclusion that when he got right down to rock bottom, he just didn't know.

Shortly after reaching that conclusion, he was walking across the village square on his way to the synagogue to pray. The cossack, or local czarist cop of this little town, was in a bad mood that morning and thought he would take it out on the rabbi. So he yelled, "Hey, Rabbi, where the hell do you think you're going?"

The rabbi answered, "I don't know."

This infuriated the cossack even more. "What do you mean you don't know where you're going?" he exclaimed in outrage. "Every morning at eleven o'clock you have crossed this village square on the way to the synagogue to pray, and here it is eleven o'clock in the morning and you're going in the direction of the synagogue and you try to tell me you don't know where you're going. You're trying to make some kind of fool out of me and I'll teach you not to do that."

So the cossack grabbed the rabbi and took him off to the local jail. And just as he was about to throw him into the cell, the rabbi turned to him and commented, "You see, you just don't know."

So I just don't know. No one does. We dwell in a profoundly mysterious universe. In the words of Thomas Edison, "We don't even begin to understand one percent about ninety-nine percent of anything."

Unfortunately, very few people realize this. Most of us think we know lots of things. We know our address and our telephone number and our Social Security number. We know how to find the way when we drive to work, and we know how to find our way back. We know that our car has something called an internal combustion engine that makes it work, and that when we turn the key in the ignition that engine will presumably start. We know that the sun rose this morning, and that it will set this evening, and that it will rise again tomorrow. So what is so mysterious?

This is the way I used to feel. When I was in medical school, I used to bemoan the fact that no more frontiers were left in medicine. All of the big diseases had been discovered and mapped out and it seemed clear that I was never going to become a Jonas Salk working late into the night making some great new discovery for the benefit of mankind.

Oh, there were a few things we realized we didn't know. A couple of months into our freshman year we students attended a presentation put on by the chairman of the department of neurology. Using a poor nearly naked man as a demonstration model in front of an amphitheater full of students, he proceeded with brilliant neuroanatomic precision to show us how this man was suffering from a lesion in his cerebellum, and another one in the upper end of his spinal cord and another down in the lower end. It was very impressive. But at the conclusion, one of my classmates raised his hand and said, "Sir, why does this man have these lesions? What's wrong with him?" And the chairman of the department of neurology puffed out his chest and declared, "This patient is suffering from idiopathic neuropathy." We all went running back to our rooms and our textbooks to look up that term and learn that idiopathic meant "of unknown cause." Idiopathic neuropathy meant nothing more than disease of the nervous system of unknown cause.

So we came to recognize there were still a few rare idiopathic neuropathies and idiopathic hemolytic anemias, and idiopathic theses and idiopathic thats we didn't quite understand yet. But all the large things were known. During my years in medical school, I often had questions, but my professors always had answers. I never once heard a professor in medical school say, "I don't know." I didn't always understand the answers, but I assumed it was my fault and it was clear that I was never—with my little brain—going to make a great medical discovery.

But about a decade after leaving medical school, I did make a great medical discovery. I discovered that we know hardly anything about medicine. I discovered it because instead of asking, "What do we know?" I began to ask, "What don't we know?" As soon as I began to ask, "What don't we know?" all of those frontiers which I thought were closed opened up. And I realized that we live in a world of frontiers.

Let me give you an example. One of those very well mapped out diseases is meningococcal meningitis, a rather uncommon but nevertheless well-known disease which afflicts perhaps one person in every fifty thousand each winter. Were you to ask any physician what causes meningococcal meningitis, she or he will tell you, "Why, the meningococcus, of course." On a certain level this is correct, because if you autopsy people who die from this dreadful disease—and about fifty percent do, while another twenty-five percent are permanently maimed—and you open their skulls, you will see that the membranes covering the brain, or the meninges, are covered with pus. Then, if you look at the pus under the microscope, you will see zillions of little bugs swimming around. And if you culture them out on the right medium, what do you find? The meningococcus, sure enough.

There is only one problem with this. Had I this past winter cultured the throats of the inhabitants of my little hometown of New Preston, Connecticut—or had I cultured the inhabitants of any northern city, such as Flint, Michigan—I would have discovered this bug in about eighty-five percent of the throats I examined. And yet no one in New Preston contracted, much less died from, meningococcal meningitis last winter, or for generations in the past, or is likely to for generations to come.

How and why is it that this bug, this bacterium which is virtually ubiquitous, can intermittently exist in 49,999 people without harm and yet can get into the brain—often of a previously healthy young person—and cause a fatal infection in but one?

The answer is: We don't know.

The same is true of virtually every disease in the

book. Let's take an unfortunately more common one, another well-known disease—cancer of the lung. We all know that smoking causes cancer of the lung. Yet there are certain people whose lips never touched tobacco and who get lung cancer and die. And there are certain people, like my grandfather, who smoked up a storm for most of his ninety-two years and never got lung cancer. So obviously, there is something in addition to smoking that is involved in the causation of cancer of the lung. And what is that something? The answer is, once again: We usually don't know.

This applies not only to virtually all diseases but also to their treatment. When I was in practice, occasionally patients for whom I prescribed certain medications would ask me, "Dr. Peck, how does it work?" And I would tell them that it alters the catecholamine balance in the limbic system of their brains. And that would shut them up. But exactly how does a certain chemical alter the catecholamine balance in the limbic system of the brain in such a way as to make a depressed person feel less depressed, or a schizophrenic think more clearly? The answer is—you guessed it—we don't know.

You may have caught on some time ago that doctors don't know much. But other people know things, don't they? I mean, medicine may be something of an art, but the hard sciences—physics, say—have all the laws pinned down.

Modern physics in many ways began with Isaac Newton, and when the apple fell on his head, he not only discovered gravity but actually developed a mathematical formula for it. So now everybody knows that two bodies attract each other with a force that is directly proportional to the product of their masses and inversely proportional to the square of the distance between them. That seems very cut-and-dried.

But why? Why do two bodies attract each other? Why should there be this force at all? What does it consist of? And the answer is: We don't know. Newton's mathematical formula simply describes the phenomenon, but why that phenomenon should exist in the first place or how it operates, we don't know. In this great age of technology, we don't even understand what it is that keeps our feet on the ground. So we haven't gotten so far with hard sciences, either.

But surely *somebody* must know something. I mentioned mathematics as very cut-and-dried. Mathematicians must know the truth. We all learned, back in school, that great truth that two parallel lines never meet. But then, along about my senior year in college, I was walking down the quad one day and I heard someone mention something about Riemannian geometry, and I found out that Bernhard Riemann was a German mathematician who, back in the middle of the nineteenth century, asked himself, "What if two parallel lines do meet?" And on the assumption that two parallel lines do meet, and a couple of other alterations that he made in Euclid's theorems, he developed a totally different geometry. This might seem like no more than an intellectual exercise or form of play, sort of like trying to figure out how many angels can dance on the head of a pin, were it not for the fact that much of Albert Einstein's work, including that which led to the development of the atomic bomb (via the theory of relativity)—which, as we all know, works—was based not on Euclidean geometry but on Riemannian geometry.

My mathematician friends tell me that the number of

potential geometries is infinite. Since Riemann's day, we have developed some six additional working geometries, so we now have a total of eight different working geometries. Which is the real one? We don't know.

PSYCHOLOGY AS ALCHEMY

Not having gotten too far with the hard sciences, let me retreat to my own "soft" science of psychology. Some have compared psychology to alchemy. Back in the days of alchemy—when scientists, such as they were, were trying to change base metals to gold—all that was known about the world was that it consisted of four "elements": earth, air, fire, and water. Since then, we have discovered the periodic table of elements and we know that there are more than a hundred fundamental elements—things like hydrogen and oxygen and carbon, and so on. But psychology still seems as if it is back in the dark ages of alchemy.

For instance, the women's liberation movement is based on certain assumptions about the nonanatomical differences or similarities between men and women. What are those nonanatomical differences and similarities? How many of them are cultural or social, and how many are biological? We don't know. Here at the end of the twentieth century, we know how to blow ourselves off the face of the earth, but we don't even begin to understand what sexuality is all about.

Or take the human trait of curiosity, very much related to this subject of mystery. Are all people born equally curious, or are people born with different curiosity levels? Is curiosity something that comes to us genetically, or is it something that we learn as we grow up in our culture? Something that is drummed into us or drummed out of us? We don't know. Once again, the dawn of a scientific body of knowledge about this most important of human traits has not yet arrived.

Knowing so little, then why is it that we humans go around thinking that we know the score, when actually we don't know beans? There are two reasons. It is because we are scared and because we are lazy.

It is scary to think that we really don't know what we're doing or where we're going, and that we are intellectual infants stumbling around in the dark. It's so much more comfortable, therefore, to live in an illusion that we know much more than we actually do.

We also live in an illusion because we are lazy. Were we to wake to the reality of our terrible ignorance, we would either have to think of ourselves as being profoundly stupid or, at the very least, let ourselves in for a lifetime of effortful learning. Since most people don't like to think of themselves as stupid or let themselves in for a lifetime of effortful anything, it's just so much more comfortable to live in this nice illusion that we know much more than we actually do.

The only problem with this is that it is an *illusion*. It is not real! You might remember in *The Road Less Traveled*, I defined mental health as a process of ongoing dedication to reality at all costs. And "at all costs" means no matter how uncomfortable the reality makes us.

Now, in our pain-avoiding culture mental health is not always encouraged. When someone suffers an emotional setback, we say, "Oh, poor Joe, he's been disillusioned." What we ought to say is, "*Lucky* Joe, he's been disillusioned." But instead we say, "Oh, poor fellow, now he sees things the way they really are, the poor guy.'' As if being made aware of reality is a bad thing. In the same way, when people come to terms, in therapy, with the fact that they were molested or abandoned as children, we can't say, ''Oh, poor person,'' because this pain they experience is ultimately health-producing.

Of course, there are exceptions to every rule, and I am a great champion of what psychologists call ''healthy illusions.'' For example, a physician who has a heart attack is probably twice as likely to die in the intensive care unit as someone who is not a physician. The reason is that he knows all the things that can go wrong, whereas someone else will say, ''Oh, I just had a heart attack!'' So sometimes illusion can be health-producing.

Yet by and large, I think it's good for us to be disillusioned. Generally, the more we are adjusted to reality, the better our lives work. But we can live in a world of reality only if we have a taste for mystery. For the reality of the situation is that our knowledge is like a little raft bobbing up and down in the sea of our ignorance, in an ocean of mystery. And people in that situation are going to be out of luck if they don't like the water. And the only way they are going to be in luck is if they love mystery, if they love to dive in it and swim in it and splash and drink it and taste it. Then they are really going to be in luck.

CURIOSITY AND APATHY

One of the things that tend to characterize the least mentally healthy, the least mature among us is their lack of a taste for mystery, or their relative lack of curiosity.

What bothers me the most when I visit a psychiatric hospital is not the insanity, not the rage or the fear or the anger or the depression, but the apathy. Sometimes it is drug-induced, but a terrible apathy often characterizes the mentally disordered.

What happens with healthy people when it begins to snow? They go to the window, look out, and say, "Hey, it's starting to snow," or, "Wow, it's really coming down heavy now," or, "Ah, it's a real blizzard out." But in a psychiatric hospital when someone says, "Hey, it's starting to snow," the patients usually respond, "Don't interrupt our card game." Or they don't want to interrupt their delusions. And they don't get up and go to the window, and they don't look out to see the mystery of the snow.

Another form that mental illness can take is when people are so unable to tolerate mystery that they may make up explanations for things that are really unexplainable. For instance, a few years ago I received a very sad eight-page letter that was quite well organized on the first page, but happened to offhandedly mention that the writer had a son with Hodgkin's disease. Then as the letter went on, the man's writing began to become considerably more disorganized. He wrote, "Of course you know, Dr. Peck, do you not, the wisdom of the ancients that we all of us have an ethereal double that goes around with us, and that there is an ionization factor that goes on between our regular bodies, our material bodies, and our ethereal doubles and disease is the result of this ionization factor?"

I did not know that. It is a possible and occasionally held esoteric theory, but it is not one for which we yet have the slightest body of evidence. So this man had in a sense found an explanation for his son's Hodgkin's disease. Perhaps it gave him some comfort in removing him from the mystery of that. But his certainty was delusional.

Conversely, one of the things that characterize the most mentally healthy among us is their great taste for mystery and their profound curiosity. They are curious about everything: about quasars and lasers and schizophrenics and praying mantises and stars. Everything turns them on. Most of us, however, fall somewhere in between total mental health and utter insanity, and for most of us, our taste for mystery lies dormant.

When I was in practice, I used to tell my patients that they were hiring me as a guide through inner space. They were hiring me not because I had ever been through their inner space before, but simply because I knew a little something about the rules for exploring inner space. In the practice of psychotherapy, everyone's inner space is different. It's a different journey each time. That's what makes it so interesting to me.

In order to explore inner space, one has to be an explorer. And to be an explorer, one has to have a taste for mystery. For Lewis and Clark, it was the mystery of what lay on the other side of the Appalachians. For astronauts it is the mystery of outer space. For patients in psychotherapy it is primarily the internal mystery of themselves. If in the course of therapy the patient's curiosity about the mystery of his early childhood was awakened, and if he began to explore forgotten memories and the influence of some experiences and events upon his life, and also the mystery of his genes and his temperament, and his heritage, and culture, and his dreams and what those dreams might mean, then therapy would go far. On the other hand, if in the course of therapy the patient's taste for the mystery of his heritage or his genes or his childhood or his dreams was not awakened, then there was no way that his journey of exploration could proceed very far.

I referred to "awakening" of the patient's taste for mystery because I believe—although we do not yet have any scientific body of knowledge to support it—that the taste for mystery is something that at least in some people can be developed, like, for example, the taste for whiskey. Except that it is an infinitely preferable taste to develop, because the more you drink in mystery, the greater the supply becomes. And no matter how much you drink, there is absolutely no hangover and it is all for free. There is no incise tax, there is no excise tax. It is the one addiction that I can heartily recommend to you.

MYSTERY AND THE SPIRITUAL JOURNEY

Living in the real world is not only the goal of mental health. It is also the goal of the spiritual journey. What is that spiritual journey, after all, but a quest to find the real meaning of life? Hopefully we are searching for the *real* God.

One of the confusing things about religion is that people go into it for different reasons. There are some who are attracted to religion in order to approach mystery, while there are others who are attracted to religion in order to escape from mystery.

It is not my intent to knock those people who use religion to escape from mystery. Because there are people who, at a particular point of their psychospiritual development (like alcoholics newly converted to AA, or criminals newly converted to a moral life), *need* some very clear-cut, dogmatic kinds of faiths and beliefs and principles by which to live. Nonetheless, it is my intent to tell you that the fully mature spiritual person is not so much a clinger to dogma as an explorer, every bit as much as any scientist, and that there is no such thing as a complete faith. Reality, like God, is something we can only approach.

In our endeavor to understand reality we are somewhat like a man trying to understand the mechanism of a closed watch. He sees the face and the moving hands, even hears its ticking, but he has no way of opening the case. If he is ingenious he may form some picture of a mechanism which could be responsible for all the things he observes, but he may never be quite sure his picture is the only one which could explain his observations. He will never be able to compare his picture with the real mechanism, and he cannot even imagine the possibility of the meaning of such a comparison.

Those words came from the pen of Albert Einstein, a man who most people would say knew more than anyone else on earth—in fact, his name has become synonymous with genius. And yet he wrote that we can observe and theorize but we can never know. Reality is something we can only approach.

One of the things that some religious people are guilty of is thinking they have God in their back pocket. But a fully mature person knows better. Reality, like God, is not something we can tie up in a nice neat intellectual little package and put in our briefcase and possess. Reality, like God, is not ours to possess. Reality, like God, possesses us.

The spiritual journey is a quest for truth as much as science is a quest for truth. The fully mature person must be a truth seeker every bit as much as the scientist is a truth seeker, and perhaps even more. Because just as some people may go into religion in order to escape from mystery, so some people will go into science in order to escape from mystery.

We all know or have heard of scientists who spend a lifetime on a study of cytochrome oxygenase in homogenate of pigeon prostate tissue at pH 3.7 to pH 3.9 and that is the extent of their interest in the universe. They have carved out a little area for themselves, and have read more papers on the subject than anybody else, so their knowledge of their area is unimpeachable, and they feel safe. But to really seek the truth, one cannot carve out a safe niche and hole up in it. One must blunder out there into the unknown, the mysterious.

In my practice, my patients would sometimes say to me, not in a psychotic way but in an ordinary existential way, "Gee, Dr. Peck, I'm so confused," and I would say, "That's wonderful!" And they would say, "What do you mean? It's awful." And I would say, "No, no, it means that you're blessed." And they would say, "What? It feels terrible. How can I be blessed?"

And I would say, "You know, when Jesus gave His big sermon, the first words out of His mouth were: 'Blessed are the poor in spirit.' " There are a number of ways to translate "poor in spirit," but on an intellectual level, the best translation is "confused." Blessed are the confused. If you ask why Jesus might have said that, then I must point out to you that confusion leads to a search for clarification and with that search comes a great deal of learning.

The people of the fifteenth century, for example, did not go to bed one night in 1492 thinking that the earth was flat only to wake up the next morning knowing that it was round. They went through a whole period of confusion and exploration when they didn't know which end was up. And for an old idea to die and a new and better idea to take its place, we have to go through such periods of confusion.

It is uncomfortable, sometimes painful to be in such periods. Nonetheless it is blessed because when we are in them, despite our feeling poor in spirit, we are searching for new and better ways. We are open to the new, we are looking, we are growing. And so it is that Jesus said, "Blessed are the confused." Virtually all of the evil in this world is committed by people who are absolutely certain they know what they're doing. It is not committed by people who think of themselves as confused. It is not committed by the poor in spirit.

In *The Road Less Traveled*, I said that the path to holiness lies in questioning everything. Seek, and you shall find enough pieces of truth to be able to start fitting them together. You will never be able to complete the puzzle. But you will be able to fit together enough pieces to begin to get glimpses of the big picture and to see that it is very beautiful indeed.

If our whole lives are embedded in mystery and we really don't know where we are going—if we are intellectual infants stumbling around in the dark—then how is it that we survive? I know of only two ways to answer that question. One is to conclude that Scott Peck and Albert Einstein are wrong, and that we know much more than they say we do. The other is to conclude that somehow we are *protected*. And that, of course, is what I have come to conclude. Now how in God's name that protection works, I have no idea except that it somehow *is* in God's name.

In my office I have the figures of seven different angels hanging around in various states of disrobement. The reason they are there is not because I have ever seen a humanoid creature with wings. But when I come to contemplate the mechanics of this protection, the mechanics of grace—how God can seemingly, literally number the hairs on our heads (which in my case is becoming less and less of a responsibility for Him these days)—I can only imagine Him having armies and legions of angels at His command.

I believe that some of these angels truly do come in human form. Phyllis Theroux wrote a collection of sparkling spiritual essays entitled *Nightlights: Bedtime Stories for Parents in the Dark*. In one of them she recounts how she once had taken a civil service exam and, typical of such examinations, there were four or five questions that were obviously designed to weed out the crazies or paranoids. She said that she could remember only one, and it asked, "Do you think you are a special agent of God?"

For a while, she recounted, she felt paralyzed, thinking of all the civil service benefits that might hang upon her answer to that question. Finally, she concluded that discretion was the better part of valor, and she picked up her pencil and lied and wrote, "No."

So I suspect that there are some special agents around, protecting us as we stumble along on our dark and mysterious journey. I particularly like to think so around the time of Halloween, that most mysterious of Christian and pre-Christian celebrations. It is then I am most likely to be reminded of that famous but anonymous seventeenth-century Scottish prayer which goes:

From ghoulies and ghosties
and long-leggedy beasties
and things that go bump in the night,
may the good Lord deliver us.

Let me paraphrase this prayer for our late-twentieth-century circumstances:

From the ghoulies of our un-understood feelings
and misunderstood hostilities,
From the ghosties of our outworn ideas to which
we cling and the illusions of our wisdom and
competence,
From the long-leggedy beasties of our ignorance
and prejudices and self-satisfaction,
And from all the things that we don't even know
enough about to be afraid of that exist in the
mysterious night beyond our limited sight,
May the good Lord deliver us—you, me, and the
whole of our struggling infant humanity.

PART TWO

The Next Step: Knowing Your Self

CHAPTER FIVE

Self-Love versus Self-Esteem

Humility is a true knowledge of oneself as one is. That is a paraphrase from a book written by an anonymous fourteenth-century monk, called *Cloud of Unknowing*. It is a profound statement, and an essential one to grasp on the search for self-knowledge.

For instance, were I to say to you that I am a lousy writer, that actually would not be humility. While not the greatest, the truth of the matter is that as people go, I am a relatively good writer. So such a statement would be what I have come to call "pseudo-humility." On the other hand, were I to tell you I was a good golfer, that would be the height of arrogance, for the fact is, I am a mediocre one at best. Genuine humility is always *realistic*.

It's critical for us to be realistic, to have a true knowledge of ourselves as we are, and to be able to recognize both the good parts and the bad parts of ourselves. Further, there is a distinction between self-love and self-esteem, in my opinion. And the difference between self-love (which I propose is a good thing) and self-esteem (which I propose can be a questionable thing) is often confused, because we really do not have accurate words for the phenomenon I am going to discuss here. I hope that eventually the problem will be somewhat solved by developing new words, but for the moment we're stuck with the old ones.

First, what do I mean by self-love?

Back when I worked as a psychiatrist in the army, the military was interested in what made successful people click, and so a dozen such people from different branches of the services were gathered together for study. They were men and women in their late thirties or early forties who had all been markedly successful. They had been promoted ahead of their contemporaries, yet they also seemed to be popular. Those who had families seemed to be enjoying a happy family life; their children were doing well in school and were well adjusted. These people seemed to have a golden touch.

They were studied in various dimensions, sometimes as a group, sometimes individually. As a part of the study they were asked to write down on a piece of paper—and they did not have the chance to consult with one another about this issue—the three most important things in their life, in order of priority.

There were two phenomena that were quite remarkable about the way the group handled this task. One was the seriousness with which they took it. The first to return his answer sheet took well over forty minutes, and a number of the people took more than an hour, even though they knew that most of the group had finished. The other thing that was remarkable was that, while the second and third items on their lists ranged all over the map, all twelve had written exactly the same answer for number one: ''Myself.'' Not ''Love.'' Not ''God.'' Not ''My family.'' But ''Myself.''

84

And that, I suggest, was an expression of mature self-love. Self-love implies the care, respect, and responsibility for and the knowledge of the self. Without loving one's self one cannot love others. But do not confuse self-love with self-centeredness. These successful men and women were loving spouses and parents and caring supervisors.

Now, what is self-esteem?

About eight or nine years after my experience with the armed forces study group, I had occasion to get close to a person of the lie—and as you might recall, I define people of the lie as essentially being evil. Such people are hard to get close to, but I got close enough to this man to ask him, "What is the single most important thing in your life?"

And what do you think his answer was? "My self-esteem."

Notice how close the answers are. The twelve successful people had written, "Myself," and he said, "My self-esteem."

I believe his answer was correct in terms of the way people of the lie function. Their self-esteem *is* the single most important thing in their lives. They will do anything to preserve and maintain their self-esteem at all times and at all costs. If there is anything that threatens their self-esteem, if there is any evidence around them of their own imperfection or something that might cause them to feel bad about themselves, rather than using that evidence and those bad feelings to make some kind of correction, they will go about trying to exterminate the evidence. And this is where their evil behavior arises. Because it is necessary for them to preserve their self-esteem at all costs.

There is a difference between insisting that we regard ourselves as important (which is self-love) and insisting that we always feel good about ourselves (which is synonymous with constantly preserving our self-esteem).

Understanding and making this distinction is crucial to our self-knowledge. In order to be good, healthy people, we have to pay the price of setting aside our self-esteem once in a while, and so not always feel good about ourselves. But we should always love ourselves and value ourselves, even if we shouldn't always esteem ourselves.

THE ADVANTAGES OF GUILT

The tool that helps us not feel good about ourselves when a self-correction is necessary is called existential guilt. We need a certain amount of guilt—a certain amount of contrition—in order to exist. Without guilt we lack an essential self-correcting kind of mechanism. If we go around thinking that we're okay all the time, then we cannot, of course, correct those parts of us that are not okay.

Most people are familiar with the book *I'm Okay, You're Okay* by Thomas Harris. It is a very good book, but I really don't like the title very much. Because what happens if you're not okay? What happens if you wake up every night at two a.m. drenched in sweat dreaming of drowning, and then you're so filled with dread that you can't get back to sleep until six a.m., and that goes on not only night after night but week after week, month after month. Is it still all right to think that you're okay?

What happens if you can't go into a store without

having a panic attack? Is it all right to think that you're okay then? What happens if you're driving your children to drugs or into serious trouble and you're not even conscious of it? Is it all right to think that you're okay?

I believe that Alcoholics Anonymous has a much better way of putting it. They have a saying "I'm not okay, and you're not okay, but that's okay."

Indeed, when I was still in the practice of psychotherapy, I used to have a certain investment in people thinking they were not okay—financial and otherwise. Because people who think they are okay do not come to psychotherapy. It is only people who think they are not okay who come, who have the humility to seek help so that they might get a head start on the journey of self-knowledge.

I cite myself as an example. About a year before I actually went into psychotherapy, I had decided that this would be a good thing for me to do. I was then a psychiatrist-in-training in the armed forces and I knew a therapist who was on the faculty of my hospital who seemed like a hip guy and would be obligated to see me for free. But when I brought up the idea to him, he asked me why I wanted to do it. So I told him, "Well, I've got a little bit of anxiety over here and a little bit of anxiety over there. It would be a useful educational experience and it would look good on my curriculum vitae." He said, "You're not ready yet," and refused to treat me.

I stormed out of his office, furious at him, but of course, he was quite right. I was not ready. I was going in feeling that I was okay. But I became ready just about a year later, to the day.

I will tell you exactly what happened on that day, but first let me tell you that, while at the time I didn't identify it as such, I was suffering from what could be called an authority problem. For the preceding twenty years, wherever I had worked or studied, there was always some son of a bitch in charge of me whose guts I absolutely hated. Always an older man. A different man each place, but wherever I went, he was there. And I thought that the problem was always that man's fault, and that it didn't have anything to do with me.

In the army at that particular time, my bête noire was the commanding general of the hospital, a gentleman I will call by the name of Smith. I hated General Smith's guts. And perhaps because I did, General Smith wasn't so kindly disposed toward me either. He must have felt the vibrations.

The day I went into therapy began with a case presentation conference, during which I had to play a tape of an interview I had conducted with a patient. My peers and one of my supervisors listened to it, and when it was over they proceeded to rake me over the coals for the clumsy, immature way I had conducted it. So the day didn't start out very well. But I was still able to maintain my self-esteem by telling myself that this was just a standard gauntlet which psychiatry residents and any psychotherapy students have to go through. They always take you to pieces, and it really didn't mean that I was inadequate or wrong in any way, shape, or form. Still, it didn't feel very good.

Then I had a little free time, and I thought I would use it to get a haircut. Now, I did not think I needed a haircut, but this was the army, and I knew that General Smith would think I needed a haircut. So, having already been criticized by my peers and my supervisor, I went off to get the haircut I didn't want.

On my way to the barbershop, I passed by the post office and decided to check my box to see if by any chance I had some mail. I did. To my dismay, I found a traffic ticket. I had gotten that ticket some two months before when I drove through a stop sign on post on my way to play tennis with the post commander, a colonel by the name of Connor—a good guy in my mind. The only problem was that when you got a ticket from the MPs on post, a copy of it always went to your commanding officer—in this case, General Smith.

Since I was already on General Smith's blacklist, I wasn't very keen about his getting something else on me, and so when I finally arrived to play tennis with Colonel Connor, in my best manipulative fashion—I was not above that sort of thing back then—I had said, "I'm sorry I'm late, sir, but I got held up by one of *your* MPs going through a stop sign trying to get here on time." He picked up on it and said, "Don't worry about it. I'll take care of it." Sure enough, the next morning, the provost marshal, or head cop of the post, called me and said, "Dr. Peck, you know that ticket that you got yesterday? Well, I just wanted to let you know that it's been lost in the mail, and next time drive more carefully." And I said, "Thank you very much, sir."

About six weeks later, however, the provost marshal was relieved of duty so summarily that he didn't even have time to clean out his desk. And when they went to clean it out, they found a whole stack of fixed tickets, which they then proceeded to redistribute. So now, having been raked over the coals by my peers and my supervisor, and on my way to get a haircut I didn't want, I found the ticket I thought had been fixed but hadn't. Feeling worse and worse, I went on to the barbershop.

About three-quarters of the way through my haircut, who should come in to get his hair cut? You guessed it. General Smith. And even though he might have wanted to, not even a general can bump someone out of a barber chair in the middle of a haircut, so he had to sit and wait his turn. And just to show you what bad shape I was in, all I could think of was: "Should I say hello to the SOB or shouldn't I? Should I or shouldn't I?" Over and over again. "Should I or shouldn't I?"

Sometimes people ask me, "When is the time to go into psychotherapy?" I say, "When you're stuck." I was stuck.

Finally, I decided to behave with great noblesse oblige and savoir faire. When my haircut was finished, I got out of the chair, and walking past him, I said, "Good morning, General Smith," then left the barbershop. Whereupon the barber came running out into the corridor saying, "Doctor, doctor, you no pay for your haircut!" So I had to come back into the barbershop, and at that point I was so nervous I dropped all my change on the floor, right at General Smith's feet. There I was, kneeling in front of him, and he was sitting literally above me, laughing at my predicament.

When I finally got out of there, I was trembling all over, and I said to myself, "Peck, you're not okay. You need help!"

THE GRACE OF BREAKING MOMENTS

That was a very painful moment—the kind of painful moment I have come to call a "breaking moment." As breaking moments go, it was really rather gentle, and that has tended to be the pattern of my life. I think God knows that I can't stand much pain.

But even though it was a very painful moment, a breaking moment, it was also one of my finest moments. Because within the hour, my still-shaking fingers were trembling their way through the Yellow Pages looking for a psychotherapist, with a genuine willingness and intent to work on myself. And painful though it was, it was the beginning of a very large growth step, a giant step forward through the desert toward salvation, toward healing for me.

Such breaking is actually symbolized in the services of the Christian churches when, at the central moment of the Communion ritual, the priest holds a piece of bread high over the altar and breaks it. A moment of breaking. And one of the things that people signify when they celebrate this ritual—whether or not they know they are doing this, and often they don't—is their own willingness to be broken. This would make Christianity seem like a very strange religion indeed—a religion of a group of people who are actually willing or want to be broken—were it not for the fact that we know it is precisely through these kinds of breakings that we are opened up, and that we make our large steps forward.

We need these moments of breaking, when we come to realize that we are not okay, that we do not have it all together, that we are not perfect, that we are not without sin. Moments of guilt, moments of contrition, moments when we are lacking in self-esteem, moments when we are bearing the trial of being displeasing to ourselves, are essential to our growth.

But even during these moments, we also need to value and love ourselves. Not only is it possible to love ourselves and realize that we are imperfect, but it's possible to do this at the same time. Indeed, often part of

our loving ourselves is the realization that there is something about us that we need to work on.

VALUABLE CARGO

About sixteen years ago, I had a patient, a seventeen-
year-old boy, an emancipated minor, who had been on
his own since the age of fourteen. He had had atrocious
parenting. I told him during one session, ''Jack, your
biggest problem is that you don't love yourself, that you
don't value yourself.''

That same night I had to drive down from Connecticut to New York in the midst of a terrible rainstorm.
Sheets of rain were sweeping across the highway and the
visibility was so poor that I couldn't even see the side of
the road or the yellow line. I had to keep my attention
absolutely glued on the road, even though I was very
tired. If I'd lost my concentration for even a second, I
would have gone off the road. And the only way I was
able to make that ninety-mile trip in that terrible storm
was to keep saying to myself, over and over again,
''This little Volkswagen is carrying extremely valuable
cargo. It is extremely important that this valuable cargo
get to New York safely.'' And so it did.

Three days later, back in Connecticut, I saw my
young patient and learned that in the same rainstorm, not
nearly as tired as I was and on a much shorter journey,
he had driven his car off the road. Fortunately, he hadn't
been seriously hurt. He had done this not because he was
covertly suicidal—although the lack of self-love can
merge into suicidality—but simply because he was not
able to say to himself that *his* little Volkswagen was
carrying extremely valuable cargo.

Let me give you another example. Shortly after *The Road Less Traveled* was published, I began treating a woman who had to travel from central New Jersey to where I live, a three-hour trip each way. She came to see me because she had read the book and liked it. She was a woman who had spent all of her life in the Christian church; she had been raised in the church and had even married a clergyman. We worked together once a week for the first year, and we got absolutely nowhere—made no progress at all. And then one day she opened the session by saying, "You know, driving up here this morning, I suddenly realized that what is most important is the development of my own soul." I broke out in a roar of joyful laughter at the fact that she had finally gotten it, but also of ironic laughter at the fact that I had assumed that this woman—who had come because she liked *The Road Less Traveled,* who was willing to make a six-hour round trip once a week to see me, and who had spent the entirety of her life in the church—already knew that what was most important was the development of her own soul. But she didn't, and I suspect that most Christians do not. Once she realized it, however, her progress in therapy was like lightning.

THE WORK OF PREPARATION

So it is terribly important that we love ourselves. Indeed, so important that I would even like to be biblical about it. Some years ago I was leading a retreat in Chicago at a huge Catholic center. The retreat was to conclude on Sunday afternoon with a formal Mass in the center's ornate church. Before the retreat began, the monk who was organizing it had asked me if I would like to give the sermon or homily at that Mass. And in a moment of unwitting stupidity and arrogance, I had said, "Oh, sure," having temporarily forgotten that in the Catholic church you cannot give a sermon on just any subject. You have to give it according to the "propers," or assigned readings for the particular day, and usually the assigned Gospel reading.

But I remembered shortly, and when I had some quiet time while the retreatants were in small groups, I picked up the Bible and found the assigned Gospel reading for that particular Sunday. It was the parable of the five wise and the five foolish virgins. I was horrified. I had never liked that parable. I had never understood it.

The parable tells of how ten virgins were hanging around waiting for the Bridegroom—Christ or God—to appear. On the chance that He might appear in the middle of the night and they might have to go out into the darkness to meet Him, five of the virgins had their lamps filled with oil, while the other five hadn't quite gotten around to it yet. Anyway, sure enough, in the middle of the night there was a knock on the door, and it was the servant announcing, "The Bridegroom's coming, the Bridegroom's coming. Come out into the night and meet the Bridegroom."

The five wise virgins immediately lit their lamps and started out the door, whereupon the five foolish virgins said to them, "Please share a little bit of your oil with us. We want to meet the Bridegroom too. Not all of your oil, not half, just a tiny bit of it." But the five wise virgins refused and proceeded out the door.

When they got to see the Bridegroom, what I had imagined He might say was, "You mean, miserable, nasty, stingy virgins! Why wouldn't you share at least a

94

little bit of your oil with those poor, less fortunate virgins?'' But that's not what He said. He said, in effect, ''Oh, you wise, wonderful, beautiful virgins, I love you, and we are going to romp in the metaphorical hay for eternity. And as far as those foolish virgins go, they can gnash their teeth and rot in Hell forever.''

The parable struck me as totally un-Christian. What on earth is Christianity about if it isn't about sharing? But I had to give a sermon on the parable, and that meant I had to think about it. Sometimes it is quite remarkable what can happen when we think. It didn't take me long to realize that the oil in this parable was a symbol for preparation, and that what Jesus was saying to us—realist that He was—was that we cannot share our preparation. You cannot do others' homework for them. Or if you do their homework, you cannot earn their degree for them, which is the symbol of their preparation. So we cannot give away our preparation. The only thing we can do—and it is often very difficult—is to try as best we can to impart to others a motive for them to prepare themselves. And I know of no way of doing that other than attempting to teach them how important they are, how beautiful and desirable they are in the eyes of God.

There is nothing that holds us back more from mental health, more from health as a society, and more from God than the sense that we all have of our unimportance, our unloveliness and undesirability. I am often amazed at how unimportant we consider ourselves to be. A decade ago I was at a dinner party where the other guests were talking about a famous film producer and how he had left his mark on history.

Suddenly I blurted out, ''We all leave our mark on

history." And that stopped the dinner table conversation dead, as if I had said something grossly obscene.

In some ways, we do not like to think of ourselves as being important. To do so would be to place responsibility upon ourselves. We like to think that the people in the Kremlin are important. The congressmen and senators in Washington are important. And if we think of ourselves as ordinary and unimportant, we can't be responsible for history, can we? But whether we like it or not, we are that important and, for better or for worse, consciously or unconsciously, we will leave our mark on history. As the expression goes, "If not you, then who? And if not now, when?"

We all have this unrealistic sense of our unimportance, of our unloveliness and undesirability. About six years ago I went to Dallas to address a scientific congress. No sooner had I picked up my key at the reception desk of the hotel than, on my way to my room, I was accosted by a young man who said, "You're Dr. Peck, aren't you? My roommate wanted to come to this conference but was unable to. But he told me that if I happened to see you I should tell you that God forgives you."

It seemed a most bizarre thing to say. But after I had settled into my room, I got to thinking about it, and I realized that there was a part of me that still felt as if I were fifteen years old, covered with pimples, utterly unlovely and inadequate and certainly no one that any scientific congress would find worth listening to. But that part of me was not a manifestation of genuine humility. It was unhealthy and unrealistic. It was in need of healing. It needed to be given up, to be forgiven and cleansed.

So, I repeat, there is nothing that holds us back more from mental health, from health as a society, and from God than the sense we all have of our own unimportance, unloveliness, and undesirability. The reality is that God is the Bridegroom and that what He is saying to us is, ''Come to bed with me. ''

But we are likely to respond, ''No, no, no, I'm too fat.''

And when God says, ''You don't understand. I love you, I want you. You are beautiful. Come to bed with me,'' we are likely to continue to shrink away, proclaiming that we are too old or too young, too unimportant or too ugly, and not worthy.

Let us prepare ourselves. Let us do so by relearning how important we are, how beautiful we are, and how we are desired beyond our wildest imaginings. And let us, as best we can, go out into the world to teach others how important they are, how beautiful they are, and how they too are desired beyond their wildest imaginings.

CHAPTER SIX

Mythology and Human Nature

T o most people, a myth is something that is untrue. But one of the advances we have made in psychiatry and psychology over the past sixty years or so—thanks largely to the work of Carl Jung and more recently to people like Joseph Campbell—is to discover that a myth is myth precisely because it is true.

Myths are stories that are found in every culture. Often they are fleshed out in slightly different ways in different cultures, but nonetheless the reason you find that same myth in culture after culture, age after age, is precisely because it embodies some great truth—virtually always about human nature. And because they have much to teach us about human nature, myths can be extremely useful for understanding ourselves.

LEGENDS

Many of the greatest archaeologists were considered in their early days to be crazy because they believed in legends or tales from the past that other people thought were not true. Perhaps the best example is that of Heinrich Schliemann. As a boy, growing up in the 1830s, he worked as an apprentice in a grocery. An elderly man used to come to eat his lunch there, and while in his cups, he would reel off verse after verse of Homer's *Iliad*. Listening to him, young Heinrich became absolutely enchanted by the story of Troy. And he vowed that when he grew up, he was going to find Troy.

When he told that to people, they said, "Oh, don't be silly. Homer's *Iliad* is just a myth. There's no such place as Troy. It's a mythical place." Nonetheless, Heinrich believed that Troy was real, and he went into business in order to make enough money to fund his search. By the time he was thirty-six, he was a very wealthy man. That was when he retired from business and went off to look for Troy. And sure enough, after about a decade, he found it, on the western shores of Turkey, proving with that and later discoveries that the stories told in the *Iliad* were not mere myths, but had a basis in fact.

Another example of such an archaeologist is Edward Thompson. At the turn of the century, Thompson heard an old Mayan legend about a well used for the drowning of virgins—who had possibly first been loaded down with gold jewelry so they would sink—as part of a sacrifice to the god of rain, who supposedly lived at the bottom of the well. And he decided he was going to find that well, even though people said, "It's just a silly legend. There's no such well. It never really existed."

Thompson went to Mexico, where he learned about a great ruined Mayan city, deep in the Yucatán jungle, called Chichén Itzá, which means "the Mouth of the Well." He bought a plantation near the ruins and soon discovered that there were two huge wells or cenotes in the area. After analyzing the ruins he guessed that the larger one, about sixty yards in diameter, might be his quarry. He then went back home to Boston, frantically raised money from all his friends, bought dredging equipment and deep-sea diving apparatus, and even learned how to dive himself.

His dredging efforts proved futile; year after year, all he and his laborers dug up was basket upon basket of mud: no gold, no bones. Just as his money was running out, after about five years of effort, he dove down himself out of desperation and found the first bones. In fact, he discovered an entire cache of archaeological remains, including a lot of gold jewelry. He recouped his borrowed fortune and his self-respect. He had proved that the legend of virgins bedecked with jewelry and thrown into a well was in fact a true story after all.

I myself did not believe in the legend of Atlantis, the island civilization said to have sunk beneath the sea. But in 1978 my father and mother took my wife and me and our three children, and my brother, his wife, and their three children on a family reunion to Greece. As part of our trip we rented a boat and sailed around a group of Greek islands known as the Cyclades. The southernmost of those islands has two names—Thera, which is its Greek name, and Santorini, an Italian name—because the Italians conquered the islands in the thirteenth century. As we were sailing toward Santorini or Thera, my father read in a guidebook that there were some people who thought that this island might be Atlantis.

I laughed at the notion. But I began to choke back my laughter as we went through what looked like a gulf between two islands and immediately saw that we had obviously sailed right into the crater of a gigantic volcano about twenty miles in diameter. As we later explored a distant part of the island rim, we learned that there, one evening in 1967, a farmer had been plowing a field with his mule while his wife and children and a neighbor's wife were standing at the edge of the field gossiping. Suddenly the farmer vanished. They didn't know what had happened to him. They ran to where they had last seen him and heard some muffled cries. There was a great hole in the ground, and they realized that he had fallen into it. Not just any hole, mind you—he had fallen into a city. It was the city of Akrotiri, buried beneath volcanic ash. As it began to be excavated, the archaeologists were introduced to an entire civilization different from any civilizations that had ever been discovered before. It dated to the Bronze Age and was a kind of blending of Greek and African cultures. It was the earliest place in the world ever to have picture windows. The discoveries there were so exciting that by the time we visited Greece a decade later, an entire new wing had already been added to the museum in Athens to house the art and other findings of Akrotiri. So I have become a believer; I have been to Atlantis.

MYTHS AND FAIRY TALES

There is a difference between a legend and a myth. Legends are tales of the past which may or may not be true. The legend of Troy is true, the legend of the Sacred Well of Chichén Itzá is true. And I think the legend of Atlantis is true. True or not, in and of themselves legends like that of the well at Chichén Itzá do not necessarily have much to teach us about ourselves. But Homer's *Iliad* is not only a true legend; it is also a myth. Woven into this story of Troy are all kinds of meanings about human nature, and that is what distinguishes a myth from a mere legend.

There is also a distinction between a fairy tale and a myth. Santa Claus is just a fairy tale, an imaginary figure who has been around for only a couple of hundred years, and is known to only about one fifth of the globe. Dragons, on the other hand, are a myth. Long before anyone ever cooked up Santa Claus, Christian monks were illuminating dragons on the margins of the manuscripts they were painstakingly copying in their European monasteries. And so were Taoist monks in China, Buddhist monks in Japan, Hindus in India, and Muslims in Arabia.

Why dragons? Why are these mythical creatures so extraordinarily international and ecumenical?

The answer is: They are human-being symbols.

They are snakes with wings. Worms that can fly. And that's us. So, reptilelike, we slink close to the ground, mired in the mud of our sinful proclivities and narrow-minded cultural prejudices. And yet like birds— or angels—we have the capacity to soar in the heavens and transcend those same sinful proclivities and narrow-minded cultural prejudices.

One of the reasons for the popularity of dragons, I think, is that they are the simplest of myths. But even so, they are not simplistic. They are multidimensional, two-sided creatures, representing a paradox. And this is one of the reasons that myths exist—to capture the multidimensional, often paradoxical aspects of human nature.

Because myths are paradoxical and multidimensional, you cannot get into trouble believing in them. However, ordinary fairy tales tend to be one-dimensional and simplistic. And you can get into a lot of trouble believing in simplistic, one-dimensional fairy tales, just as simplistic thinking about anything in our lives can get us into trouble. Simplistic thinking afflicts all of us. We want things black and white. We want things to be either one thing or another, when, in fact, every aspect of our lives is at least two things simultaneously, if not half a dozen things.

For example, when I lecture, certain Christians in the audience sometimes ask me, ''Dr. Peck, should homosexuals be ordained as priests?'' They ask this question as if homosexuality were just this or just that, when, as far as I can ascertain from my limited psychiatric experience, there are some people who are homosexual by virtue of having grown up in extremely dysfunctional families (and therefore have a condition theoretically treatable, albeit only with difficulty), and there are other people who are homosexual, I am convinced, genetically, and whom God created homosexual. And then there are all kinds of mixtures in between, people who are homosexual as a result of both biological and psychological determinants. So when we regard homosexuality as just this or just that, we do violence to the subtlety and complexity of God's creation. The answer to the question ''Should homosexuals be ordained?'' is the same as to the question ''Should heterosexuals be ordained?'' It depends on the homosexual. It depends on the heterosexual.

THE MYTH OF RESPONSIBILITY

Myths are a wonderful source of learning about the paradoxical, multidimensional, complex aspects of human nature. You might recall that in *The Road Less*

Traveled, I mentioned the myth of Orestes, the son of Clytemnestra and Agamemnon. According to Homer, Clytemnestra took a lover and together they murdered Agamemnon. This put Orestes in what might be called a bit of a bind. The greatest obligation a young Greek boy had was to avenge his father's murder. Yet it was his mother who was responsible in this case. And the worst thing a Greek boy could possibly do was to murder his mother.

Orestes murdered his mother and her lover, thus avenging his father's death. But then he had to pay the price and was cursed by the gods with what were called the Furies, three harpies who continually surrounded him, cackling in his ear, giving him hallucinations, driving him to madness. For years and years, Orestes went around the world atoning for what he had done, while the Furies pursued him. Finally he asked the gods to relieve him of their curse. So a trial was held at which the god Apollo, who was Orestes' defense attorney, argued that the whole fiasco was the fault of the gods. Because Orestes hadn't really had any choice in the matter, consequently he should not be blamed for what he had done.

Whereupon Orestes stood up and countered Apollo. "It was I, not the gods, who murdered my mother," he said. "It was I who did this."

Never before had any human being assumed such total responsibility for his behavior, when he could have blamed it on the gods. Hearing this, the gods deliberated and decided to lift the curse from Orestes. The Furies were transformed into the Eumenides, which means literally "Bearers of grace." Instead of being cackling, nasty, negative voices, they became voices of wisdom.

This myth represents the transformation of mental illness into extraordinary health. And the truth that the price of such a marvelous transformation is accepting the responsibility for ourselves and our behavior.

THE MYTH OF OMNIPOTENCE

Another revealing myth I spoke of in *The Different Drum* is that of Icarus. Icarus and his father sought to escape from prison by building wings of feathers and wax for themselves. When Icarus took flight, he wanted to keep flying to reach the sun. But of course, as soon as he even began to get near the sun, the heat melted his self-made wings and he plummeted to his destruction.

One of the meanings of this myth is the folly of attempting to assume godlike powers. The sun is often a symbol for God. Another meaning of the myth, I think therefore, is that we cannot get to God under our own power. We can get to God only with God pulling us up. And we can get into trouble, we can plummet to our destruction, if we think otherwise.

This is one of the problems people encounter when they discover "spiritual growth," and first fully realize they are on a spiritual journey. They start to think that they can direct it. They think if they go off to a monastery for a weekend retreat or take some classes in Zen meditation, or take up some Sufi dancing, or attend an EST workshop, then they'll reach nirvana. Unfortunately, that is not the way it works. It works only when God is doing the directing. And people can get into a certain kind of trouble—like Icarus—if they think they can do it on their own.

If you think you can plan your spiritual growth, it

ain't going to happen. I don't mean to discount workshops or other forms of self-inquiry—they can be valuable. Do what you feel called to do, but also be prepared to accept that you don't necessarily know what you're going to learn. Be willing to be surprised by forces beyond your control, and realize that a major learning on the journey is the art of surrender.

THE MYTHS IN THE BIBLE

What is the Bible? Is it literal truth? Is it a collection of myths? Is it merely some outdated rules? What is it? And what relevance does it have in our lives?

I'm reminded of a woman who said to me, "I had great trouble dealing with the Bible as long as I thought of it as a book of orthodoxy. But then I suddenly realized one day that it is a book of paradoxy, and ever since then I have absolutely loved it."

Indeed the Bible is a collection of paradoxical stories, and as befits a collection of paradoxes, it is itself paradoxical—it is not just one thing. It is a mixture of legend, some of which is true and some of which is not true. It is a mixture of very accurate history and not so accurate history. It is a mixture of outdated rules and some pretty good rules. It is a mixture of myth and metaphor.

How are we to interpret the Bible? Although they place such importance on it, the fundamentalists, in my experience, strangely misuse the Bible. Actually, the term "fundamentalists" is a misnomer. The more proper term is "inerrantists," those who believe that the Bible is not only the divinely inspired word of God but the actual transcribed, unaltered word of God, and that it is subject to only one kind of literal interpretation, namely theirs. Such thinking, to my mind, only impoverishes the Bible.

I once heard Wayne Oates, one of the two founders of the pastoral counseling movement, speaking of this problem in terms of a young man who had gouged out one of his eyes because Jesus said, "If your eye offend you, pluck it out." And Wayne said, "You know, I'm a good old Southern Baptist boy, and I dearly love my Lord Jesus, but I sure as hell wish He had never said that."

The problem isn't with what Jesus said. The problem is that this young man took what He said literally. Jesus, of course, was speaking metaphorically. He did not mean for you to cut off your arm or gouge out your eye. What He meant was that if there is something in your way, something that stands between you and mental health or spiritual growth, you should get rid of it. Don't sit around complaining about it.

So the Bible is not always meant to be interpreted literally. A great deal of it is metaphor and myth, subject to a variety of complex, and often paradoxical, interpretations.

THE MYTH OF GOOD AND EVIL

Among the most complicated and multidimensional is Genesis 3, the myth of Adam and Eve in the Garden of Eden. Myths, like dreams, can work by what Freud called condensation. A single dream can have condensed into it not just one but two or three different meanings. This certainly applies to the myth of the Garden of Eden. It is an extraordinary story that contains not just one profound truth, not two, not three, but more than a dozen profound truths to teach us about human nature.

Although the fundamentalists—the inerrantists and creationists—may not like it, one of the things that the Eden myth teaches us about is evolution. This doesn't mean that God didn't have a hand in evolution; indeed, I think that He/She very much did. Specifically, Genesis 3 is a myth about how we human beings evolved into consciousness. I have already spoken in the first chapter of some of the consequences of this evolution, so pointedly elucidated through this great story: our shyness, our self-consciousness, our sense of separation from nature, and our need to continue evolving into ever greater consciousness. Now let me note that with consciousness comes the awareness of good and evil.

So another thing this wonderfully rich story teaches us is about the power of choice. Until we ate the apple from the Tree of the Knowledge of Good and Evil, we didn't have real choice. We did not have free will until that moment described in Genesis 3 when we became conscious, and having become conscious, we were faced with the choice of going after the truth or going after the lie. Thus the Eden story also has a great deal to do with the whole genesis of good and evil. You can't have evil unless you have choice. When God allowed us free will, He inevitably allowed the entrance of evil into the world.

It so happens that another, even earlier myth, Genesis 1, also has something to say about evolution as well as good and evil. It tells how God first created the firmament, and then the land and the waters, and then the plants and the animals. It is the same sequence as that suggested by geology and paleontology. As far as scientists can determine, that is the sequence of evolution, even though we can't say it all happened in seven days.

A whole new meaning to Genesis 1 occurred to me when I remembered that God first created light and He looked at it and saw that it was good. So He created the land and saw that it was good. And so He separated the land and the water and saw that that was good too, so He went on to create the plants and the animals. And when He saw that they too were good, He then created human beings. Thus, I think the impulse to do good has something to do with what creativity is all about.

Similarly, the impulse to do evil is destructive rather than creative. The choice between good and evil, creativity and destruction, is our own. And ultimately, we must take that responsibility and accept its consequences.

THE MYTH OF THE HERO

Joseph Campbell has done much to teach us about the truth that resides in myths. One of the great myths of the world which Campbell has been particularly effective in elucidating is called "The Myth of the Birth of the Hero," from his book *The Quest of the Hero*. As is typical of myths, this one appears in slightly different variations in different cultures, but nonetheless its bare bones are the same. There is always a sun god and a moon goddess who mate, and they produce a child who is always a boy. (Perhaps we can alter this little piece of the story as time goes by.) In growing up, the boy goes through a period of great struggle and turmoil and pain, from which he emerges as a hero.

What does this myth mean? First, let me explain

what a hero is. A hero is defined as the person who can solve a problem or problems that other people can't. Let's say, for example, there is a king who has a wonderful country, or it would be wonderful if it weren't for this mean, miserable, nasty dragon that's making everybody's life difficult. So the king decides that whoever can slay the dragon will get the hand of the beautiful Princess Esmerelda in marriage. Word travels throughout the land, and one by one the bravest Harvard- and Yale-educated knights of the realm come out to do battle with the dragon, and one by one they get eaten. The situation becomes truly dire and all seems lost, when out of the woods of the Bronx there comes a young Jewish man educated at NYU who has a certain kind of smarts. He figures out how to slay the dragon and does. The king isn't necessarily terribly happy about having a Jewish son-in-law; nonetheless he is true to his word. So the young man marries the beautiful Princess Esmerelda, and they live happily ever after in a wonderful country.

This young man, therefore, is the hero because he solved the problem that others couldn't: in this case, how to slay the dragon. But how did he come by such smarts? Remember that the true hero, according to the myth, must be the offspring of the sun god and the moon goddess. Thus this myth is also about masculinity and femininity, because, typically, the sun god and the moon goddess symbolize masculinity and femininity.

We have long been fascinated by the masculine/feminine dichotomy, in legend and in life. For example, a very popular area of inquiry these days is the relationship of the right brain and the left brain to different kinds of thinking. As that would apply to the "myth of the birth of the hero," the sun god stands for masculinity, for light and reason and rational scientific knowledge—namely, analytic left-brain kind of thinking. And the moon goddess stands for femininity, for darkness and feeling and intuition—namely, the right-brain kind of thinking. Having mated, these two have produced a child that has both the sun god and the moon goddess in him—or her. So then, this is a myth about what we call *androgyny*.

The obvious conclusion is that we can become heroes only if we learn how to use both our femininity and our masculinity—our left brain and our right brain. This is something that very few people ever learn to do. Instead, most of us, as we are growing up, learn to emphasize our masculinity at the expense of our femininity, or to elevate our femininity at the expense of our masculinity. Or we may learn how to approach certain kinds of problems in a masculine, left-brained sort of way, and certain other kinds of problems in a feminine, right-brained sort of way. But very seldom do we learn how to approach the same problem with both our right brain and our left brain.

This integration of our masculinity and our femininity is achieved very painfully. It is the struggle that the child goes through in the myth in the course of his or her growing up. But if we can go through this struggle of integration and learn how to approach the same problem with both our right brain and our left brain simultaneously, with both our masculinity and our femininity, then we too can be heroes. We too will be able to solve problems that the world has not yet been able to solve—a world that is desperately in need of heroes and solutions.

THE CHOICE OF INTERPRETATION

Let me return to the matter of the Bible and emphasize how often we have a choice of how to interpret its stories. We can always interpret them literally. Take, for instance, the story of Lot's wife, also in Genesis. When God destroyed the sinful cities of Sodom and Gomorrah, He permitted Lot and his wife to flee on the condition that they not look back. But Lot's wife did look back and she was instantly turned into a pillar of salt. Taken literally, this is simply a story of the kind of punishment we will receive and what can happen to us if we disobey God.

Over the past hundred years there has developed a new school of "scientific" biblical interpretation. It proposes "rational" explanations for the miraculous happenings described in the Bible—like the parting of the Red Sea—suggesting, for instance, that there are places where the Red Sea is very shallow and when the conjunction of the tides is just right once every hundred years or so, it can actually be waded across. This school has also had its hand in the story of Lot's wife. So the story is footnoted in the New Oxford Bible with the comment that it is an "old tradition to account for bizarre salt formations in the area such as may be seen today on Jebel Usdun."

But this supposedly scientific explanation somehow left me feeling cold. So I got to thinking more about it and wondering why God had not wanted Lot or his wife to look back. What is wrong with looking back? Then I got to thinking about people who spend much of their lives looking back—in regret—and what can happen to them when they become obsessed with the past. And it dawned on me that such people become essentially pickled, as if they had turned into a living pillar of salt. With this metaphorical interpretation, I began to see in the story of Lot's wife deep meaning and a profound statement about human nature.

I sometimes tell people that one of the great blessings of my life was an almost total absence of religious education, because I had nothing to overcome. I say "almost" because I did go to Sunday school for one day. For some reason, when I was eight and my brother was twelve, my parents decided that we needed a religious education. So they packed us off to Sunday school, and I can remember the day very well, because I had to color a picture of Abraham sacrificing Isaac. Perhaps I was a bit of a psychiatrist even back then, because I quickly concluded that God must be crazy for wanting Abraham to kill his son, and that Abraham must have been crazy for even thinking about doing it. And above all, Isaac must have been crazy for just lying there in my coloring book with this beatific expression on his face, waiting to be sliced open.

As it turned out, my brother refused to go back, and with his twelve-year-old power, he was able to make that stick. So I rode his twelve-year-old coattails out of Sunday school, and that was the extent of my religious education. And I still do not think the story of Abraham and Isaac is appropriate for eight-year-olds, because—if you subscribe to Jean Piaget's stages of mental development—children of that age tend to think concretely or literally and have not yet developed much capacity for interpretation. But just as there can be the wrong age for a story, so can there also be a right age and a correct time for interpretation.

Now that I am in late middle age, the story of Abraham sacrificing Isaac has profound meaning for me. I believe it is a most important story for all of us with children who are adolescent or older. Interpreted metaphorically, this wonderful story—or myth—teaches us that the time comes when we have to give up our children. Yes, they were gifts to us and given unto our keeping—but not forever. Holding on to them beyond a certain point can be extremely destructive to them, and ourselves as well. We need to learn how to return the gift and entrust our children to God. They no longer belong to us. They are God's children now.

CHAPTER SEVEN

Spirituality and Human Nature

People sometimes ask me the most impossible questions—for example, "Dr. Peck, what is human nature?" And because my parents raised me to be an obliging child, I try to come up with answers to such impossible questions, and the first answer I give is: "Human nature is to go to the bathroom in your pants."

It really is. That is exactly the way each one of us started out, doing what came naturally and letting go whenever we felt like it. But then what happened along about the time we were two years old or so, our mother or possibly our father—although usually it is our mother who gets the message across—came to us and said, "Hey, you're a nice kid and I like you a lot, but I'd kind of appreciate it if you would clean up your act."

Initially, such a request makes absolutely no sense whatsoever to the child. What makes sense is to do what comes naturally and let go whenever one feels like it. Moreover, the result is always interesting and different each time. Sometimes it comes in a form that you can write on the walls with, and sometimes it's in hard little balls you can toss out of the crib and watch bounce on the floor. But it makes absolutely no sense to do what is profoundly *unnatural*, which is to keep a tight fanny and somehow manage to get to the bathroom just in time to see this beautiful stuff flushed away and put to no useful purpose.

However, if there is a good relationship between the child and its mother, and the mother is patient and not too demanding or too controlling—and unfortunately, these circumstances often are not met, which is why psychiatrists are so into toilet training—but if these circumstances are met, the child says to itself: "You know, Mommy is a nice old gal and she's been awful good to me these last couple of years, and I'd like to do something to pay her back. I'd like to give her some kind of gift of my appreciation. But I'm just a puny, helpless two-year-old, so what could I possibly have to give her that she might want or need—except this one crazy thing?"

So the child—as a gift to its mother—starts doing the unnatural and keeping that tight fanny and going to the toilet. But look what happens here over the next few years. Something absolutely marvelous. By the time the child reaches the age of four or five, if in a moment of stress or fatigue it forgets and has an accident, it feels unnatural about the messy business whereas it has come to feel utterly natural about going to the toilet. In this brief span of time, as a gift of love to its mother, the child has changed its nature.

INSTINCT AND HUMAN NATURE

So the other response I most commonly make when people ask me, "Dr. Peck, what is human nature?" is to say there is no such thing. And that, above all else, is our glory as human beings.

What distinguishes us humans most from other creatures is not our opposing thumb, or our wonderful larynx which is capable of speech, or our huge cerebral cortex, but it is our dramatic relative lack of instincts or preformed, preset inherited patterns of behavior, which give other creatures a much more fixed nature than we have.

I live in Connecticut on the shores of a large lake and to that lake, every March when the ice melts, there comes a flock of gulls, and every December when the lake freezes over, the gulls depart, presumably for parts south. I never used to know where they went, but some friends have recently told me that it's Florence, Alabama.

Whether there are migratory gulls or not, scientists who have studied migratory birds have come to realize that they are actually able to navigate by the stars. They have built into them—through heredity—complex patterns of celestial navigation which enable them to land in Florence, Alabama, right on the dot every time. The only problem is that there is no particular freedom about it. The gulls can't say, ''I think this winter I'd like to spend in Bermuda or the Bahamas or Barbados.'' It's either Florence, Alabama, or nothing.

What distinguishes us human beings, on the other hand, is the extraordinary freedom and variability of our behaviors. Given the wherewithal, we can go to the Bahamas or Bermuda or Barbados. Or we can do something totally unnatural and, in the middle of winter, go north to Stowe, Vermont, or to the mountains of Colorado and slide down icy hills on little slats of wood or fiberglass. This extraordinary freedom to do the different and often seemingly unnatural is the most salient feature of our human nature.

Nowhere was this better described than in *The Sword in the Stone* by T. H. White. To paraphrase and condense a tale from this wonderful book, it was back in the very early days, when all of the earth's creatures were still in embryonic form. God called all the little embryos together one afternoon and said, "I'm going to give each of you whatever three things you want. So come up here one by one and ask for whatever three things you want and I will give them to you."

So the first little embryo came up and said, "God, I'd like to have hands and feet in the shape of spades so I can dig myself a safe home underneath the ground, and I'd like to have a thick, furry coat to keep me warm in the winter, and I would like to have some sharp front teeth so I can chew on the grasses."

And God said, "Fine, go and be a woodchuck."

Then the next little embryo came up and said, "God, what I like is the water, and I'd like to have a flexible body so I can swim around in it. I'd also like to breathe underwater with some kind of gills, and I'd like a system that will keep me warm no matter what the temperature of the water is."

And God said, "Fine, go be a fish."

God went through all the little embryos until there was just one left, which seemed to be a particularly shy little embryo—perhaps for the same biblical reasons I've already discussed. It was so shy that God had to motion it forward and ask, "All right, last little embryo, what three things would you like?" And it said, "Well, I don't want to seem pre-presumptuous or anything. It's not that I'm not . . . ah . . . grateful, because I am. But . . . but I was wondering if maybe . . . if it was all right with You . . . I could stay just the way I am—an embryo.

118

Maybe sometime later when I'm smart enough to know the three things I really want, I can ask You for them then. . . . Or maybe . . . if You want me to become a certain something, you can give me the three things that You think I need.''

And God smiled and said, ''Ah, you are human. And because you have chosen to remain a perpetual embryo, I will give you dominion over all of the other creatures.''

Of course, most of us throw our embryohood away. As we get older, we become set in our ways, fixed in our nature. Watching my parents and other people as they entered their fifties and sixties, it invariably seemed to me when I was young that they became less interested in new things, more and more convinced of the rightness of their own opinions and worldviews.

Indeed, that was the way I thought it had to be, until I reached twenty. During the summer of that year, I went to live with the noted author John Marquand, who was sixty-five at the time, and he blew my mind. I found that this sixty-five-year-old man was interested in everything, including me, and no sixty-five-year-old had ever been seriously interested in unimportant little twenty-year-old me before. He and I used to argue late into the night most evenings, and I could actually win some of those arguments. I could actually change Mr. Marquand's mind. In fact, by the end of the summer, I would see Mr. Marquand changing his mind about three or four times a week. I realized that this man, rather than having grown old mentally, had grown younger, and was more open and more flexible than most children or adolescents.

It was at that point, for the first time, I realized that we do not have to grow old mentally. We do have to grow old physically. All of us will eventually become decrepit and die, but most of us do not have to stop growing mentally. So it is that—while we may usually toss it away—this capacity for ongoing change and transformation is the most salient feature of our human nature.

THE STAGES OF SPIRITUAL GROWTH

Our unique human capacity for change and transformation is reflected in our human spirituality. Throughout the ages, deep-thinking people looking at themselves have come to discern that we are not all at the same place spiritually or religiously. There are different stages of spiritual growth or religious development. The person best known today for writing on the subject is Professor James Fowler at the Candler School of Theology at Emory University, author of, among others, a book called *Stages of Faith.*

Fowler describes six stages of spiritual growth, which I have refined into four, but we are saying essentially the same thing. His work is much more scholarly than mine, filled with academic references to the works of other stage theorists such as Piaget, Erikson, and Kohlberg. I arrived at my own understanding of these stages not out of book learning but through experience—in particular, several of what I've come to call "noncomputing" experiences. The first of these occurred about the time I was fifteen when I decided to visit some of the Christian churches in my area. To some extent I was interested in checking out what this Christianity business was all about, but primarily I was interested in checking out the girls.

The first church I decided to visit was just a few

blocks down the street, and it had the most famous preacher of the day, a man whose Sunday sermons were broadcast over every radio wavelength in the land. At the age of fifteen, I had no trouble spotting him as a phony. However, I also went up the street in the opposite direction to another church which also had a well-known preacher, although not nearly as famous as the first. His name was George Buttrick, and at the age of fifteen, I had absolutely no trouble spotting him as a holy man, a true man of God.

My poor fifteen-year-old brain didn't quite know what to make of this. Here was the most famous Christian preacher of the day, and as far as I could see at fifteen, I was already well ahead of him in my spiritual growth. But then, in the same Christian church, there was another preacher who was obviously light-years ahead of me. It didn't seem to make any sense, didn't seem to compute, which is one of the reasons I turned my back on the Christian church for the next twenty-five years or so.

Another one of those noncomputing experiences occurred more gradually later in my life. After I had been practicing psychotherapy for some years, a strange pattern began to emerge. If religious people came to see me because they were in pain and trouble and difficulty, and they really got involved in therapy, then—more often than not—they would leave therapy as questioners, doubters, skeptics, agnostics, possibly even atheists. But if atheists or agnostics or skeptics came to me in pain, trouble, and difficulty and they really got involved in therapy, then—more often than not—they would leave therapy having become deeply religious or spiritually concerned people.

This pattern just made no sense, did not compute. Same therapist, same therapy, successful yet utterly opposite results. I couldn't figure this out, until it slowly began to dawn on me that we are not all at the same place spiritually and that there are these different stages. We must look at them with caution and flexibility, however, because God has this rather peculiar way of interfering with my categories sometimes, and people do not always fall quite as neatly into my psychospiritual pigeonholes as I might like them to do.

At the beginning—the bottom, if you wish—is Stage One, which I label "chaotic/antisocial." This stage probably encompasses about twenty percent of the population, including those whom I call people of the lie. In general, this is a stage of absent spirituality and the people at this stage are utterly unprincipled. I call it antisocial because while they are capable of *pretending* to be loving, actually all of their relationships with their fellow human beings are self-serving and covertly, if not overtly, manipulative. Chaotic because, being unprincipled, they have no mechanism that might govern them other than their own will. Since the unharnessed will can go this way one day and that way the next, their being is consequently chaotic. Because it is, the people in this stage will frequently be found in trouble or difficulty, and often in jails or hospitals or out on the street. Some of them, however, may actually be quite self-disciplined, from time to time, in the service of their ambition and may rise to positions of considerable prestige and power. They may even become presidents or famous preachers.

The people in Stage One may occasionally get in touch with the chaos of their own being. And when they do, it is perhaps the single most painful experience a human can have. Generally, they just ride it out, but if this painful experience continues, they may kill themselves, and I think that some unexplained suicides may fall into this category. Or occasionally, they may convert to Stage Two. Such conversions are usually—I say usually because there are always exceptions—very sudden and dramatic. It is as if God literally reaches down and grabs that soul and yanks it up in a quantum leap. Something astonishing happens to that person and it is usually totally unconscious. If it could be made conscious, I think it would be as if that person said to himself or herself, "I am willing to do anything—*anything*—in order to liberate myself from this chaos, even submit myself to an institution for my governance."

And so it is that they convert to Stage Two, which I have labeled "formal/institutional." I label it institutional because people in it are dependent upon an institution for their governance. For some the institution may be a prison. In such places, in my experience, there is always a prisoner who, when the new psychiatrist comes in to work in the prison, gathers a group of fellow inmates together for a group therapy session, who is the warden's right-hand man, yet who somehow manages never to get a shiv stuck between his ribs. He is a model prisoner and a model citizen. Because he is so well adjusted in the institution, he is always paroled at the first possible opportunity. Immediately he becomes a walking crime wave, and within a week of his parole, he is rearrested and put right back behind bars, where once again he becomes a model citizen with the walls of the institution around him to organize his being.

For others the institution may be the military. This is a profoundly positive role the military plays in our and other societies. There are tens of thousands of people who would lead chaotic lives were it not for the rather paternalistic and in some ways maternalistic structuring of the military.

For still others, the institution to which they submit themselves for their governance may be a highly organized business corporation. But for most people, it is the church. Indeed, the majority of churchgoers fall into Stage Two, the formal/institutional stage. Although there are gradations and nothing is absolutely cut-and-dried within these stages, certain things tend to characterize people's religious behavior in Stage Two. As mentioned, they are dependent on the institution of the church for their governance, and I call it formal because they are very attached to the forms of the religion.

Stage Two people become very, very upset if someone starts changing forms or rituals, altering their liturgy or introducing new hymns. For example, in the Episcopal church, in the mid-seventies, it was decided that there might be some alternative ways to say the same things on different Sundays, and many people were so up in arms that a full-blown schism resulted. Another example: In the 1960s, the Vatican II Council of the Roman Catholic hierarchy led to profound changes in that church, and thirty years later Pope John Paul II still seems to be in the process of trying to undo those changes. And it's not just Episcopalians and Catholics. This kind of turmoil goes on in every denomination of every religion in the world. And it's no wonder that people in Stage Two become so upset when the forms of their religion are changed, because it's precisely those forms that they depend upon to some extent for their liberation from chaos.

Another thing that tends to characterize people's religious behavior in this stage is that their vision of God is almost entirely that of an external being. They have very little understanding of that half of God which lives inside each of us—what theologians term immanent—the dwelling divinity within the human spirit. They almost totally think of God as up there, out there. They generally envision God along the masculine model, and while they believe Him to be a loving being, they also ascribe to Him a certain kind of punitive power which He is not afraid to use on appropriate occasions. It is a vision of God as a giant benevolent cop in the sky. And in many ways, this is exactly the kind of God that people in Stage Two need.

Let's say that two people who are firmly rooted in Stage Two meet and marry and have children. They raise their children in a stable home because stability tends to be of great value to people in Stage Two. They treat their children with dignity and importance because the church says that children are important and should be treated with dignity. And while their love may be a little bit legalistic or unimaginative at times, nonetheless they are loving because the church tells them to be loving and teaches them a little something about how to be loving.

What happens to a child raised in such a stable, loving home and treated with dignity and importance? That child will absorb his parents' religious principles—be they Christian, Buddhist, Muslim, or Jewish—like mother's milk. By the time the child reaches adolescence, these principles will have become virtually engraved on his heart, or "internalized," to use the psychiatric term. But once this happens, they will have become principled, self-governing human beings who no longer need to depend upon an institution for their governance. It is at this time, which in healthy human development is usually at adolescence, that they start saying, "Who needs these silly myths and superstitions and this fuddy-duddy old institution?" They will then begin—often to their parents' utterly unnecessary horror and chagrin—to fall away from the church, having become doubters or agnostics or atheists. At this point they have begun to convert to Stage Three, which I call "skeptic/individual."

Again speaking generally, people in Stage Three are ahead of people in Stage Two in their spirituality, although they are not religious in the ordinary sense of the word. They are not the least bit antisocial. Often they are deeply involved in society. They are the kinds of people who tend to make up the backbone of organizations like Physicians for Social Responsibility or the ecology movement. They make committed and loving parents. Frequently they are scientists, and certainly scientific-minded. Invariably they are truth seekers. And if they seek truth deeply enough, and widely enough, as I've suggested, they do begin to find what they are looking for, and get to fit enough pieces of truth to catch glimpses of the big picture and see that it is not only very beautiful, but that it strangely resembles many of those primitive myths and superstitions their Stage Two parents or grandparents believed in. And it is at this point that they begin to convert to Stage Four, which I call "mystical/communal."

I use the word "mystical" to describe this stage even though it is a word that is hard to define and one that has been given a pejorative connotation in our culture and is usually misdefined. But certain things can be said about mystics. They are people who have seen a kind of cohesion beneath the surface of things. Throughout the ages, mystics have seen connections between men and women, between humans and other creatures, between people walking the earth and those who aren't even here. Seeing that kind of interconnectedness beneath the surface, mystics of all cultures and religions have spoken of things in terms of unity and community. They also have always spoken in terms of paradox.

Mystical has as its root the word *mystery*. Mystics are people who love mystery. They love to solve mysteries, and yet at the same time, they know the more they solve, the more mystery they are going to encounter. But they are very comfortable living in a world of mystery whereas people in Stage Two are most uncomfortable when things aren't cut-and-dried.

These principles hold true not only for Christianity and not only in the United States but in all nations, cultures, and religions. Indeed, one of the things that characterize all of the world's great religions is that they seem to have a capacity to speak to people in both Stage Two and Stage Four as if the very teachings of a given religion have two different translations. To take an example from Judaism, Psalm 111 ends with ''The fear of the Lord is the beginning of wisdom.'' At Stage Two this is translated to mean, ''When you start fearing that big cop in the sky, you really wise up.'' That's true. At Stage Four it is translated to mean, ''The awe of God shows you the way to enlightenment.'' And that's also true.

''Jesus is my Savior'' is a favorite statement among

127

Christians and provides another example. Among Stage Two people, that tends to be translated to mean that Jesus is a kind of fairy godmother who can rescue me whenever I get in trouble as long as I can remember to call upon His name. And that's true; He will do exactly that. Whereas in Stage Four, people read it to mean that Jesus, through His life and death, taught me the way that I myself must follow for my salvation. And that is also true.

As I noted, this quality of dual translation holds true not just for Christianity and Judaism but also for Islam, Taoism, Buddhism, and Hinduism. Indeed, I think it is what makes them great religions. They all give room for both the Stage Two and the Stage Four believers.

ANTAGONISM AND FAITH

The greatest problem of these different stages—and the biggest reason it is so important to understand them—is the sense of threat that exists between people at such different points on the spiritual journey.

To some extent, we all may be threatened by the people still in the stage we have just left, because we may not yet be sure or secure in our new identity. But for the most part the threat goes the other way, and we particularly tend to be threatened by people in the stages ahead of us.

People in Stage One will often tend to appear like cool cats—seemingly nothing bothers them very much. But if you are able to penetrate that facade, you find they are terrified of virtually everything and everyone.

People in Stage Two are not particularly threatened by the Stage One people: the sinners. They *love* the sinners, seeing them as fertile ground for their ministrations. But they tend to be threatened by the skeptic individualists of Stage Three, and more than anything, by the Stage Four people, who seem to believe in the same things they believe in and yet believe them with a kind of freedom they find absolutely terrifying.

Stage Three people, the skeptics, are not particularly threatened by the unprincipled people of Stage One, or by the Stage Two people, whom they simply toss off as superstitious idiots. But once again, they tend to be threatened by the Stage Four people, who seem to be scientific-minded like them and know how to write good footnotes, yet still somehow believe in this crazy God business. And if you mentioned the word "conversion" to the Stage Three people, they would see a vision of a missionary arm-twisting a heathen and they would go through the roof.

I have used the word "conversion" rather freely to describe the transition from one stage of spirituality to the next. It is, however, a markedly different experience in each case. Conversions from Stage One to Stage Two are usually very sudden, very dramatic. Conversions from Stage Three to Stage Four, on the other hand, tend to be gradual. For example, I was in the company of Paul Vitz, the author of *Psychology as Religion*, when he was asked when he had become a Christian. He scratched his head and said, "Well, it was along about somewhere between '72 and '76." Compare that to the Stage Two man who says, "It was eight p.m. on the night of the seventeenth of August!" Obviously, a different sort of phenomenon is going on here.

I have also spoken of Stage Three people—the skeptics and doubters—as being spiritually ahead of the vast majority of churchgoers of Stage Two. These people have also undergone a "conversion"—that is, a conversion to skepticism and doubt, which is something equivalent to what the Bible calls a "circumcision of the heart." They are ahead of the Stage Two man who acknowledges Jesus to be his Lord and Savior at exactly eight p.m. on the night of the seventeenth of August, but may yet have to undergo a conversion to peace or to justice. Conversion is not a onetime thing. Like any kind of spiritual growth, it is a continuing process. I expect and hope to continue to be converted until the day I die.

APPEARANCES CAN BE DECEIVING

I'd like us to be reminded at this point how God can interfere with my categories, and how we need to be both cautious and flexible when we make diagnoses of where our fellow humans—and we ourselves—fall in this spectrum of spiritual growth. There are quite a number of people who superficially appear to be in one stage when, in fact, they are someplace else entirely. For example, there are people who attend church and who, to the naked eye, appear to be in Stage Two, but who inwardly are dissatisfied with their religion and are skeptical of it and have become scientific-minded. This is so common that entire congregations have been created which are only faintly religious. A lot of Methodist and Presbyterian ministers in wealthy suburban communities don't talk to their congregations about God on Sunday mornings, but about psychology. God forbid they should talk about God. It would be too threatening. Then again, there are people who talk about God but are not the least bit religious or spiritual. These are people who may appear to be in Stage Four, who can wear Stage Four veneer—like certain cult leaders—but who, in fact, are Stage One criminals.

Similarly, not all scientists are Stage Three people. They too know how to write good footnotes, but only in an extremely narrow area of research where they have the scientific doctrine down so pat that they feel very safe while ignoring all the mystery of the world. Such scientists are really Stage Two people.

There are also people whom psychiatrists refer to as borderline personalities. One of the things that characterize them is that they seem to have a foot in Stage One and a foot in Stage Two, and a hand in Stage Three, and a finger in Stage Four. They're all over the place. They lack coherency, and that, in a sense, is why we call them borderline: they don't have much in the way of borders or boundaries.

Furthermore, there are people who might begin to enter a more advanced stage, then slip backwards. We actually have a name for the person who slips back from Stage Two to Stage One—"backslider." Typically, he might be a man who ran around drinking and gambling and chasing after women and leading a dissolute life, until one day he bumped into some fundamentalist folk who had a chat with him and he was saved. For the next couple of years, he leads a sober, God-fearing, righteous life and then he vanishes one day, and nobody knows where he is until six months later when he is discovered back in the gutter or gambling house. His church friends talk with him and he is saved again and does pretty well for another couple of years, until he backslides once more.

There are also people bouncing back and forth between Stage Two and Stage Three. An example of such a person might be a churchgoer who says, "Of course I still believe in God. I mean, look how beautiful nature is—those hills turning green and the white clouds flying and the flowers blooming. Obviously, no human intelligence could have created such beauty, so there must have been a divine intelligence that set all this in motion millions and millions of years ago. But you know, it's just as beautiful out on the golf course as it is in church on Sunday morning and I can worship my God out on the golf course just as well."

So this man chooses the golf course over church. And all is well, until his business undergoes a mild reversal and he says, "Oh my God, I haven't been going to church! I haven't been praying!" He goes back to church and starts praying very hard, until after a couple of years there is an upturn in the ecomony—for all I know perhaps because he's been praying so hard—and he begins to drift back onto his Stage Three golf course.

Then there are people bouncing between Stage Three and Stage Four. I had a friend like that named Theodore. By day Theodore had an absolutely brilliant scientific mind with a precisely honed rational capacity, and was probably just about the dullest human being I ever had to listen to. But occasionally in the evening Theodore would have a little bit to drink or he would smoke a little bit of pot and all of a sudden he would start talking about life and death and meaning and glory. He would become so spirit-filled that I would sit at his feet enthralled. But the next morning he would come in to see me and say, "I don't know what got into me last night. I was talking about the craziest things. I've got to stop drinking or smoking pot." I do not mean to bless the use of drugs but simply to indicate that in his particular case, they seemed to loosen him up enough to flow in the direction in which he was being called, but from which, in the cold clear light of day, he would retreat in abject terror right back into his accustomed Stage Three rationality.

HUMAN DEVELOPMENT AND SPIRITUAL GROWTH

While it is possible when we are not yet firmly rooted to backslide, it is not possible for us to skip over any of the stages of spiritual development, any more than it is possible to skip over any of the purely psychological stages of normal human development. And in fact, these two patterns of growth follow a similar progression. For example, children up until the age of five or so are pretty much Stage One creatures. They haven't yet internalized the difference between right and wrong, and they will lie, cheat, steal, and manipulate with abandon. It's hardly remarkable that many of them grow up to be adult liars, cheats, thieves, and manipulators. In fact, it's harder to explain how so many of them grow up to be honest, decent, law-abiding folk.

From about the age of five to twelve, children tend to be Stage Two creatures. They may be mischievous, but they're not seriously rebellious. Basically, they think that the way Mommy and Daddy want things to be done is the way things ought to be done. They are great imitators and followers. But with adolescence, all hell breaks loose. Everything that Mommy and Daddy say— which always used to be like the word of God—is now subject to rebuttal and rejection. This is the stage of individual questioning and of skepticism. And Stage Four cannot begin until adolescence has been worked through.

If none of the stages can be skipped over, movement through certain stages can proceed more swiftly for some people than for others. For instance, I have a friend who was raised in a Stage Two Irish Catholic home, and when he was fifteen, just as he was entering his adolescent rebellion period, his father's company transferred the family to Amsterdam. There my friend was sent to a Dutch Jesuit school. The Dutch Jesuits are very sophisticated people. Indeed, one of Pope John Paul II's enduring problems has been to figure out how to excommunicate all of Holland, because the entire country leans remarkably toward a Stage Four culture. So my friend fell into the hands of these sophisticated and accepting Jesuits, who encouraged his doubt, and led him in his doubting. When he came back from Amsterdam at the age of nineteen, he was already in early Stage Four.

While it is possible to move quickly through the stages, it is also quite possible to get stuck. Years ago when I was a consultant to a convent, I interviewed their postulants before they were clothed as novices, the first very formal process of determining whether one is really cut out to be a monk or nun. I remember one such postulant in particular, a woman in her mid-forties, whom I was asked to interview because the novice mistress was concerned about her; while she was an ideal postulant, the other postulants and novices just didn't like her that much.

As I was interviewing this woman, it hit me that it

was not like having a forty-five-year-old woman in my office. Her carriage and manner were more like those of a slightly silly eight-year-old girl. When I asked her about her spirituality, what I heard didn't sound original. It sounded like some good little girl reeling off her well-learned catechism. Being a psychiatrist, after a while I said, of course, "Tell me about your childhood."

And she said, "Oh, I just had a wonderful, wonderfully happy childhood." This naturally made me suspicious immediately, because no one has had a wonderful, happy childhood. So I said, "Go on, what was so wonderful about it?" She then told me that she had a sister who was just a year older than she was, and that they were very close and used to play all the time. The sister had invented a ghost called Oogle, and one time she and her sister were in the bathtub together and her sister exclaimed, "Watch out! Oogle is coming!" So she ducked underneath the water to get away from Oogle, and her mother beat her. I asked her why and she said, "Because I got my hair wet."

Then I learned that her mother had gotten multiple sclerosis when this postulant was twelve, and died when she was eighteen. How can you have an adolescent rebellion against a woman who not only would beat you for getting your hair wet but also has a fatal illness at the time when you ordinarily begin your adolescence, and dies before you're old enough to sort it out? If you can't have an adolescent rebellion, you will likely become fixated in Stage Two. That is what had happened to this woman.

CHECK YOUR DUNGEON

Another important thing to know about the stages of spiritual growth is that no matter how far we develop, all of us retain vestiges of earlier stages, just as we retain our vestigial appendix. There is a Stage One segment lurking down in the dungeon of my personality—Scott Peck, the criminal—although I don't intend to let him get out. Indeed, it is only because I recognize his existence that I can add another cinder block to his cell every week or so. Nonetheless, it is a very comfortable cell. It's got wall-to-wall carpeting and a color TV, and sometimes in the evening when I'm in need of certain kinds of street smarts, I may go down to that dungeon and talk with him, keeping well to the other side of the bars.

Similarly, there is a Stage Two segment to my personality—the Scott Peck who also in times of stress or strain would very much like to have a big brother or big daddy around to give him some clear-cut, black-and-white answers to life's difficult and ambiguous dilemmas, who will take over the responsibility by providing me with formulas to tell me exactly what I should do. Sometimes I keep him on bread and water.

And similarly, there is a Stage Three Scott Peck, who in certain other times of stress tends to regress and is tempted to lean on his scientific side as opposed to relying on his spiritual side. I used to tell people that if I was ever invited to address the American Psychiatric Association—of which the chances were like a snowball's in Hell—I would probably just talk about controlled studies and not say anything about this immeasurable spirit business. But the truth of the matter is that I *was* invited to speak to the American Psychiatric Association and I generally managed to throw the Stage Three Scott Peck right into the dungeon along with the Stage One Scott Peck.

Make no mistake about it. We all retain within us, no matter how far we develop, vestiges of earlier stages of our spirituality. So if you are feeling smug right now, having convinced yourself you are safely walking the righteous path of Stage Four, check your dungeon. Conversely, if you're feeling either superior or inferior, it might be helpful to realize that we all also contain within us traces—the lurking potential—of the more advanced stages. As Oscar Wilde once put it, "Every saint has a past and every sinner a future."

There is another reason for some humility in this matter. The first time I ever talked about these stages was at a seminar with Paul Vitz, whom I have already mentioned as one of the nation's authorities on the integration of psychology and religion. During the period he had for rebuttal after I had spoken, Paul said, "I was very interested in hearing about Dr. Peck's stages. I think there is a great deal of validity to them. Indeed, I think that I will be using them myself in my own practice of psychotherapy. But I would like all of you to remember that what Scotty calls Stage Four is the beginning."

CHAPTER EIGHT

Addiction:
The Sacred Disease

I must confess that I am an addict. In particular, I am almost hopelessly addicted to nicotine. I write and lecture all about self-discipline, yet I don't have enough of it myself to stop smoking.

Having put that admission behind me, let me point out that drug and alcohol abuse and addiction are multifaceted, multidimensional problems. While I am going to consider here only the psychological and spiritual aspects of addiction, I am well aware that there are profound biological and sociological roots as well. Alcoholism is a genetic, inherited disorder. We know that now. But that doesn't mean that because you have a gene for alcoholism you will become an alcoholic, or that once you become one you have to continue drinking. It does mean, simply, that there are biological roots to this disorder.

Similarly, although not yet as well studied, it seems to me that there are obviously biological determinants to the kinds of drugs one might prefer, and become addicted to. For example, while not quite addicted, I happen to be partial to alcohol and other sedative drugs, all of which are called central nervous system depressants.

In other words, I like downers. I don't give a fig for uppers. But I know people who could kill for uppers and don't care in the least about downers. There are also sociological determinants to addiction. Drug abuse is most severe in places of sociological hopelessness, where people have no better way to feel good about themselves than getting high.

One way of looking at addictions is to see them as forms of idolatry. For the alcoholic the bottle becomes an idol. And idolatry comes in many different forms, some of which we're quite accustomed to recognize. So there are nondrug addictions, such as addictions to gambling or sex. The idolatry of money is another. Idolatry also comes in forms we are not accustomed to recognize as readily. One is the idolatry of family. Whenever it becomes more important to do or say what will keep the family matriarch or patriarch happy than it is to do or say what God wants you to do or say, we have fallen prey to the idolatry of family. Family togetherness has become an idol, and often a most oppressive one.

To put things in perspective, therefore, it is important for us to keep in mind that there are innumerable kinds of idolatries or addictions, many of which can be far more dangerous than the addiction to drugs. The addiction to power. The addition to security. In some ways, drug and alcohol addictions may be among the least destructive of addictions or idolatries in terms of their overall cost to society.

With that by way of introduction, let us now restrict ourselves to the consideration of the problem of drug addiction alone. I think that people who become slaves to alcohol and other drugs are people who want, who yearn, to go back to Eden—who want to reach Paradise, reach Heaven, reach home—more than most. They are desperate to regain that lost warm, fuzzy sense of oneness with the rest of nature we used to have in the Garden of Eden which I spoke about in the first chapter. So it is that Kurt Vonnegut's son, Mark, in writing about his own mental illness and drug abuse, entitled his book *The Eden Express*. But of course, one cannot go back to Eden. One can only go forward through the painful desert. The only way to reach home is the hard way. But addicts, who have a terribly powerful yearning to go home, are going the wrong way—back instead of forward.

There are two ways of looking at this yearning to go home. One is to look at it as a regressive kind of phenomenon, a yearning not only to go back to Eden but to crawl back into the womb. The other way to look at it is as a potentially progressive kind of phenomenon; that in this yearning to go home, addicts are people who have a more powerful calling than most to the spirit, to God, but they simply have the directions of the journey mixed up.

JUNG AND AA

Few people know that Carl Jung—who did more than anyone else to marry psychology with spirituality—actually played an indirect role in the founding of Alcoholics Anonymous. Jung had a patient back in the 1920s, an alcoholic man who after about a year of therapy had made no progress. Finally Jung threw up his hands and said to him, "Listen, you're just wasting your money with me. I don't know how to help you. I can't help you." And the man asked, "Is there no hope for me then? Nothing you can suggest?" And Jung said, "The only thing I can suggest is that you might seek a religious conversion. I have heard reports of a few people who underwent religious conversions and stopped drinking. It makes a kind of sense to me.''

The man took Jung at his word and went out seeking a religious conversion. Seek and you shall find? Well, he found it. After about six years, he underwent a religious conversion and stopped drinking.

Shortly after it happened, he bumped into one of his old drinking buddies, a man by the name of Ebby, and Ebby said, ''Hey, have a drink.'' But he said, ''No, I don't drink anymore.''

Ebby was astonished. ''What do you mean, you don't drink anymore? You're a hopeless alcoholic, just like me.'' So the man explained that Jung had told him to seek a religious conversion, and that he had stopped drinking.

Ebby thought that might be a good idea. So he went out looking for a religious conversion. It took him about two years. And he too stopped drinking for a significant period.

Not long after that, Ebby dropped in one night to see his old drinking buddy Bill W. Bill W. said, ''Hey, Ebby, have a drink.'' But Ebby said, ''No, I don't drink anymore.'' Now it was Bill W.'s turn to be astonished, ''What do you mean, you don't drink anymore? You're a hopeless alcoholic, just like me.'' So Ebby recounted how he had met this patient of Jung's who had undergone a religious conversion and stopped drinking, and how he had done the same thing.

Bill W. thought that was a good idea. So he too went out looking for a religious conversion. It took him a couple of weeks, and shortly thereafter he started the first AA meeting in Akron, Ohio.

141

About twenty years later, once it had really gotten off the ground, Bill W. wrote to Jung to tell him about the role he had inadvertently played in the founding of AA. And Jung wrote back to him an absolutely fascinating letter. He said he was terribly glad that Bill W. had written to him; he was glad to know that his patient had done well; he was glad to know the role he had inadvertently played. But he also said he was particularly glad because, while there were not many people that he, Jung, could talk to about such things, it had occurred to him that it was perhaps no accident that we traditionally referred to alcoholic drinks as spirits, and that perhaps alcoholics were people who had a greater thirst for the spirit than others, and that perhaps alcoholism was a spiritual disorder, or better yet, a spiritual condition.

Thus, there are two ways to look at this yearning that addicts have to go home, and both are true. It would be wrong to totally disregard the regressive aspects of addiction, but nonetheless, in working with people, I have found that the greatest payoff generally comes in emphasizing the positive. So in dealing with addicts, the greatest payoff comes from emphasizing not the regressive aspects of the disorder but rather the progressive ones—the yearning for the spirit and for God.

A PROGRAM OF CONVERSION

When I was in psychiatry training, back some thirty years ago, psychiatrists already knew that Alcoholics Anonymous had a much better track record in working with alcoholics than we psychiatrists had. But we dismissed it as nothing more than a substitute for the neighborhood bar. We believed that alcoholics had what we called "oral personality disorders," and that rather than opening their mouths to drink, they would get together at AA meetings and yap a lot and drink a lot of coffee and smoke a lot of cigarettes, and in that way they would satisfy their "oral" needs. That was the reason, we psychiatrists smugly said, that AA worked.

I am ashamed to tell you that the majority of psychiatrists, including those who are training right now, continue to believe that the reason AA works is because it is a substitute addiction. I do not want to say that there is no element of this. "Substitute addiction" is perhaps one half of one percent of the reason AA works so well. But the real reason AA works is because of "the program." And there are at least three reasons why the program works.

The first reason is that the twelve steps of AA are the only existing program for religious conversion, although AA people call it "spiritual" conversion, because they do not want in any way to imply that AA is an organized religion. It is not. However, the very core of the twelve-step program is the concept of higher power, and the program actually teaches people why they should go forward through the desert—namely, toward God "as we understand Him."

Because it is the only program for conversion, AA might be looked upon as the most successful "church" in this country today. Any other denomination would envy its extraordinary, phenomenal growth. AA people are incredibly smart. They're so smart that they don't even bother about budgets and buildings. In fact, they use existing church buildings for their meetings. This is one of the positive roles the institutional church plays today—it hosts AA meetings.

About a year ago I was speaking in a modest-sized church in a Connecticut town, and during the break time I looked at the bulletin board and saw that that church hosted some fourteen AA meetings each week, along with four Al-Anon meetings and two Overeaters Anonymous meetings.

So, while AA people will use church buildings for meetings, they are not affiliated with organized religion. They will also soft-pedal even the "spiritual" aspect of the program in order to attract new members who are threatened by it. And lots of people are threatened by it. People simply don't like to be converted very much. They resist it. Consequently, AA is a very tough program.

To give you an idea of how tough it is, an alcoholic executive came to see me about a dozen years ago because "AA wasn't working." By that he meant that for the past six months he had been going to AA meetings every other night, and on alternate nights he had been continuing to get blind drunk. He said he didn't know why AA wasn't working, because he understood all about the twelve steps.

When he told me that, I said with some surprise, "As far as I understand the twelve steps, they are a rather profound body of spiritual wisdom, and it usually takes people at least three years to even *begin* to be able to comprehend them."

He then acknowledged that maybe there was something to what I was saying, because certainly he didn't understand anything about all this higher power stuff. But he was sure that he understood at least the first step.

And I said, "Oh, what's that?"

"I've come to admit that I'm powerless over alcohol."

So I prodded him on. "What does that mean?"

"That means I've got this kind of biochemical defect in my brain such that whenever I take a drink, the alcohol takes over and I lose my willpower. So I can't take that first drink."

"Why are you still drinking, then?"

He fell silent and looked confused.

And I said, "You know, maybe the first step means not only that you are powerless over alcohol after you've taken that first drink, but that you're powerless over alcohol even before you've taken that first drink."

He shook his head vehemently. "That's not true. It's up to me whether or not I take that first drink."

"That's what you say, but it's hardly how you're behaving, is it?"

But he kept insisting, "It's still all up to me."

So I said, "Well, have it your way, then."

This executive had not yet undergone the surrender required of the very first of the twelve steps, much less the remaining eleven.

A PSYCHOLOGICAL PROGRAM

The second reason AA works is that it is a psychological program. It teaches people not only *why* to go forward through the desert toward God but also a great deal about *how* to go forward through the desert. It teaches this in two primary ways.

One is through the use of aphorisms and proverbs. I have already mentioned a few of them, "Act as if," and "I'm not okay and you're not okay, but that's okay." But there are many others—all marvelous gems: "The only person you can change is yourself." Or "One day at a time."

I will tell you a personal story of why I am so convinced that proverbs are important. I had the kind of grandfather every boy ought to have. He was not a particularly smart man, and his speech was seldom more than a series of clichés. He would say to me, "Don't cross your bridges until you've come to them," or, "Don't put all your eggs in one basket." Not all were admonishments; some were consoling, like, "It's often better to be a big fish in a little pond than a little fish in a big pond," or, "All work and no play makes Jack a dull boy."

He was not above repeating himself, however. If I heard "All that glitters is not gold" once, I must have heard it a thousand times. But he loved me. And from the time I was about eight or nine years old until the time I was thirteen, once a month I used to travel across Manhattan Island to spend a weekend with my grandparents. The ritual of those weekends never varied. I would arrive there on Saturday morning in time for my grandmother to serve me lunch, and then after lunch—this was before the days of TV—my grandfather would take me to a double-feature movie and sit with me through it. Then we would go home for dinner, and after dinner, my grandfather would take me to a second double feature. On Sunday morning the movie theaters were closed in deference to God, but Sunday afternoon he would take me to a third double feature before sending me home. And that was love.

It was on the walks with my grandfather, back and forth to the double features, that I was able not only to hear but to digest and absorb his proverbs, and their wisdom has stood me in very good stead over the years. As he himself might have put it, "A spoonful of sugar helps the medicine go down."

146

Years later when I was practicing psychiatry, a fifteen-year-old boy came to see me, referred from his local prep school because of poor grades. And as I talked to him, he struck me as not being terribly bright. I thought that maybe the reason he had poor grades was because he was stupid. We psychiatrists have a way of assessing intelligence as part of what we call a "mental status exam," and one of the parts of that exam is to ask people to interpret proverbs. So I asked him, "Why do people say, 'People who live in glass houses shouldn't throw stones?' "

He immediately answered, "If you live in a glass house and you throw stones, your house is going to break."

"But most people don't really live in real glass houses. How would you apply that saying to relationships between people?"

"I don't know."

I tried again. "Why do people say, 'Don't cry over spilt milk'?"

And he said, "If I spilled some milk, I'd get the cat in to lick it up."

That seemed somewhat imaginative, but didn't explain why it was a common expression. Finally, because intelligence was such a critical issue, I referred him to a psychologist for tests that are much more accurate in assessing intelligence, and I specifically referred him to an elderly woman particularly famous in the testing field. I was surprised when her report came back demonstrating that this boy had a full-scale IQ of 105. Not great, and low for that prep school, which might have explained something about his poor grades, but still above average. I would have assessed his IQ at about 85, and because of the discrepancy, I called her and said that I couldn't believe his IQ was 105, that I was sure it had to be much lower since he did so badly on proverbs. "Oh, we don't worry about that," she said. "None of the young people these days know any of the old proverbs anymore."

I've often thought that it would be saving if we could develop some program of mental health education in our public schools, but I know we wouldn't get away with it. People would object to it. There is an anti-mental health movement in this country consisting of people who are frightened by the influences of secular humanism and psychology movements in our lives. They are horrified that someone would think that it is good for children to talk back to their parents, and they consider that this kind of thinking has to be the work of the devil. But even they couldn't possibly object to a program in our schools to teach the old proverbs to our children, could they? So I hope someone will start instituting such a program.

I also hope it will be done soon. For, as my grandfather would have said, "A stitch in time saves nine."

LAY PSYCHOTHERAPY

AA uses proverbs very effectively and it also has another effective mechanism: a system of sponsors. When you join AA or another twelve-step program, after a while you may choose a sponsor, who is really a lay psychotherapist.

If you feel you need psychotherapy but you can't afford it, then one thing you could do is to pretend you're an alcoholic, go to AA, and get yourself a sponsor. There are actually some people who do that. I'm not into pretense, so that isn't what I would really recommend. Instead, I would suggest that you pretend you've got an alcoholic relative and go to Al-Anon and get yourself a sponsor. Actually, you don't have to pretend. Undoubtedly somewhere in your family you do have an alcoholic relative.

I don't mean to imply that sponsors in the twelve-step programs are the exact equivalent of paid-for, professional psychotherapists. In some ways they're not as good. The reason I know as much as I do about AA is because I have had patients who came to me after spending years in the program, feeling that maybe I had a little something extra I could give them as a psychiatrist that they couldn't get from their sponsors. In the process of trying to give them that little extra boost, I learned a great deal from them.

There is something of a tradition in the twelve-step programs that it is really okay to outgrow your sponsor. And, in this respect, I believe the sponsor system superior to traditional therapy. It's considered normal to go to your sponsor and say, "Look, I'm really grateful for the help you've given me for the past three years, but I think at this point I'm ready for a more sophisticated sponsor." And the sponsor is likely to say, "I couldn't agree with you more, and I'm delighted that I've been able to help you and that you've come this far." There are not that many psychiatrists who would take as kindly to their patients' outgrowing them.

A COMMUNITY PROGRAM

Thus, AA works because it is a program of spiritual conversion, teaching people *why* they must go forward through the desert—namely, toward God. And it works because it is a psychological program, teaching people a great deal about how to go forward through the desert, and it does so through proverbs and sponsors. There is a third reason: AA works because it teaches people that they do not have to go forward through the desert alone. It is a *community* program.

For the past several years, since I gave up practicing psychiatry, I have been working with others on the development of the Foundation for Community Encouragement. My book *The Different Drum* was all about that effort. In it I pointed out that community develops naturally only in response to crisis. So it is that strangers in the waiting room of an intensive care unit will rapidly come to share with each other their deepest fears and joys, because their relatives lie across the hall on the critical list. Or within a few hours of an earthquake, like the one in 1985 in Mexico City, where over four thousand people were killed, normally self-centered, wealthy adolescents will be working hand in hand with poor laborers in around-the-clock sacrificial love.

The only problem is that as soon as the crisis passes, so does the community. As a result, there are millions of people who are mourning their lost crises. I can guarantee you that this Saturday night, if not this Thursday night, there will be tens of thousands of old men in VFW and American Legion clubs drinking themselves silly, mourning the days of World War II. They remember those days with such fondness because even though they were cold and wet and in danger, they experienced a depth of community and meaning in their lives that they have never quite been able to recapture since.

150

THE BLESSING OF ALCOHOLISM

Alcoholics in AA have a great blessing and a great genius.

The blessing is the blessing of alcoholism. It is a blessing because it is a disease which visibly breaks people. Alcoholics are not any more broken than people who are not alcoholics. We all have our griefs and our terrors; we may not be conscious of them, but we all have them. We are all broken people, but alcoholics can't hide it anymore, whereas the rest of us can hide behind our masks of composure. We are not able to talk with each other about the things that are most important to us, about the way our hearts are breaking. So the great blessing of alcoholism is the nature of the disease. It puts people into visible crisis, and as a result they get into community—an AA group.

The great genius of alcoholics in AA is that they refer to themselves as recovering alcoholics. They do not refer to themselves as recovered alcoholics, or ex-alcoholics, but recovering alcoholics. And by using that word ''recovering'' they are constantly reminding themselves that the process of recovery is ongoing, the crisis is ongoing. And because the crisis is ongoing, the community is ongoing.

One of the worst problems I have in my work with the Foundation for Community Encouragement is trying to explain to people what it is about. The only people who get it right away are those in the twelve-step programs, because to them I can say that the Foundation for Community Encouragement tries to teach people how to get into community without having to be an alcoholic first, without having to have a crisis first. Or better yet, it is trying to teach people that they are—we all are—already in crisis.

151

MEETING CRISES EARLY

In our pain-avoiding culture, we have a very strange attitude toward mental health. We Americans think that what characterizes the mentally healthy is an absence of crises. *That is not what characterizes mental health!* What characterizes mental health is the ability to meet our crises early.

The word "crisis" has become quite fashionable these days; we are all talking about the midlife crisis, for example. But long before we ever coined that term, we spoke about the midlife crisis in women. It was menopause. Many women, when they reached their fifties and their period stopped, tended to fall apart. But curiously, it didn't happen to all women, and I can tell you why.

A mentally healthy woman does not face a big midlife menopausal crisis at fifty-six, because she has handled many small crises along the way. At age twenty-six, for example, she wakes up one morning and looks in the mirror and sees that she's got the beginning of crow's feet at the corner of her eyes. That's when she's apt to think to herself, "You know, I'm not really sure that a Hollywood talent scout is going to come around after all." And ten years later when she's thirty-six and her youngest child goes off to kindergarten, she thinks, "You know, maybe I'm going to have to do a little more with my life than focus it on my children." When such a woman reaches her fifties and her period stops, she will sail right through it. Other than a few hot flashes, she will have absolutely no trouble because psychologically she met her menopause twenty years before.

The woman who gets into trouble, on the other hand,

is the one who holds on to the fantasy that a Hollywood talent scout is going to come around, and who doesn't develop any interests outside the home. When fifty hits, which is the time her period stops, and which is also the time no amount of makeup can hide the wrinkles any longer, and which is also the time her children leave home—leaving her with not only an empty nest but an empty life—it is no wonder that she falls apart.

I do not want to stereotype either women or menopause here, because midlife crisis is just as common and just as severe in men. I know. Not long ago, I went through my third midlife crisis. I was more depressed than I've been at any time since the age of fifteen, and it hurt. I just want to make the point clearly that what characterizes mental health in both men and women is not measured by how well we can avoid crises, but how early we can meet a crisis and can get on to the next one—and perhaps how many crises we can cram into a lifetime.

There is a rare, devastating form of psychological disorder afflicting perhaps one percent of the population which impels them to lead lives of compulsive theatricality. They have to have excitement all the time. But the far more devastating psychological disorder which afflicts at least ninety-five percent of us Americans is that we fail to live our lives with a sufficient sense of drama and to wake up to the critical nature of our lives on a daily basis.

Herein lies one of the virtues of being a "religious" person. Other people simply have ups and downs in their lives, whereas we religious folk get to have "spiritual crises." It is much more dignified to have a spiritual crisis than a depression. In fact, it is quite possible that

153

you will get over your depression more quickly if you recognize it to be a spiritual crisis, which very often it is. One of the things that I deeply believe we need to do in our culture is to start dignifying crises, including certain types of depression and all types of existential suffering. It is only through such suffering and crisis that we grow.

AA people, because they are always recovering, live with ongoing crisis. And they cope with ongoing crisis because they help each other. That is what community is.

I am able to tell you what community is, but I cannot tell you how it feels. Jesus had a similar problem. He had stumbled on this thing He called the Kingdom, and got very excited about it. But when He tried to describe it to people, their eyelids drooped and they would yawn. So He made up parables to explain Himself better. He would say: "Look, it's like a man who has found a pearl of great price." Or, "It's like a man who had a vineyard and needed some workers." Or, "It's like a man who had a prodigal son." By and large they still didn't understand what He was talking about.

Two thousand years later, even though His parables have become the most famous of literature, people still don't understand what He was talking about. Most Christians don't really understand what is meant by the Kingdom. I think it is no accident that Jesus had the same kind of difficulty talking about the Kingdom that we have talking about community. Because I think the Kingdom is the closest analogue there is to community.

You have heard Jesus quoted as saying that "the Kingdom is within you," but actually that is not what He said. Jesus was speaking Aramaic and the Gospels were written in Greek and then translated into every language known to man. So there were bound to be mistakes, and there have been thousands of books written trying to get at the correct translations and the actual words of Jesus.

One of the ways that scholars have found to test the accuracy of a Gospel passage is to see if it is possible to translate the Greek back into Aramaic. Most scholars now agree that Jesus did not say "the Kingdom is within you." He said "the Kingdom is among you." And I believe that the best way we find the Kingdom is among us is in community.

In his book *The Scent of Love*, Keith Miller writes about this very thing in terms of the first followers of Jesus. It has been said that the early Christians were such phenomenally successful evangelists because the Holy Spirit came down and gave them various gifts—of charisma and of tongues—so that they could speak all languages, and thus Christianity spread like crazy. But Miller suggests that that wasn't the major reason.

What really happened was that, through Jesus, the disciples and early followers had discovered the secret of community. Someone would be walking down a back alley in Ephesus or Corinth and see people sitting together talking about the strangest things that didn't make any sense at all: something about a man and an execution on a tree and visitations. But there was a quality about the way these people talked to each other, cried together, laughed together, touched each other, the way they interacted with each other, so oddly compelling that strangers passing by would be drawn to them. It was as if the scent of love had drifted down the alley and could draw people like bees to a flower. And people started to say, "I don't understand this yet, but I want in."

We've done community-building workshops in the most sterile of hotel rooms, and desk clerks and barmaids would come by and say, "I don't know what you're doing here, but I get off at three—can I join you?" So I have an idea how it might have worked.

Thus I believe the greatest positive event of the twentieth century occurred in Akron, Ohio, on June 10, 1935, when Bill W. and Dr. Bob convened the first AA meeting. It was not only the beginning of the self-help movement and the beginning of the integration of science and spirituality at a grass-roots level, but also the beginning of the community movement.

That is the other reason why I think of addiction as the sacred disease. When my AA friends and I get together, we often come to conclude that, very probably, God deliberately created the disorder of alcoholism in order to create alcoholics, in order that these alcoholics might create AA, and thereby spearhead the community movement which is going to be the salvation not only of alcoholics and addicts but of us all.

PART THREE

The Ultimate Step:
In Search of
a Personal God

CHAPTER NINE

The Role of Religion in Spiritual Growth

I am very cautious about my use of "religious" words. I often talk about spirituality rather than religiosity, for example, or about higher power instead of God. I am cautious because these words may have negative connotations. One of the great sins of organized religion is that it has tended to corrupt some very holy words. And when people encounter these words, they associate them with the hypocrisy of organized religion and can no longer see or hear their real meaning.

Many of us have been harmed by religion. And when I talked about the necessity of forgiving your parents for the sins they committed in your childhood, I should have also said that it is equally important to forgive your church for the sins it may have committed in your childhood. Forgiving does not mean going back. I am not telling you to go back to the church of your childhood, any more than I would tell you to move back home with your parents. But your spiritual growth demands that you forgive nevertheless. Without such forgiveness you cannot begin to separate the true teachings of that church from its hypocrisy. And you need the true teachings.

A book called *Oneness: Great Principles Shared by*

All Religions carries the following quotation from the Dalai Lama on its cover.

> Every major religion of the world has similar ideas of love, the same goal of benefitting humanity through spiritual practice, and the same effect of making their followers into better human beings.

Inside, you find that the founders of every major religion in the world—among them Jesus, Buddha, Krishna, Confucius, and Muhammad—have all taught the notion of loving one's neighbor. Wherever you might choose to anchor your spirituality—be it in Christianity, Judaism, Hinduism, Taoism, Buddhism, or Islam—you will have to accept these basic truths. Because you need these basic truths as signposts on your own spiritual journey. Which religion that should be I cannot tell you, because each of us is unique.

INDIVIDUAL UNIQUENESS

I am constantly impressed by how different people are. I am impressed with the different gifts they possess. I have no idea whether God creates the uniqueness in their souls before they're born, or whether it is in their genes. I do know that it starts from the word go.

My two daughters were clearly different beings by the time Lily and I brought them home from the hospital. Had we just had a boy and a girl, we might have said, "They're different because of their sex." But having two of the same sex really brought it home dramatically that we had, right from birth, two very different beings.

People are born different, and among the problems

they have to solve is how to deal with their own uniqueness, their own differences, and come to terms with that in relation to other people. Being different, we each have our own special vocation, our own special calling. We each have a will, the mysterious freedom of choice which operates within certain biological limitations and the confines of one's particular gifts. The one thing I regret in *The Road Less Traveled* is that I made the journey sound like a template clearer than it actually is. As I reread that book, I am amazed by the depth of truth that was given to me, but a bit dismayed by a certain glibness I no longer seem to have. I did not take into account all the variety that exists out there.

There's great benefit in variety. This variety of people is part of what makes community and it is necessary to make up a whole. We need variety to be whole. There is also a great variety of roads that we can take. Because each of us is unique, we have our own choices to make. And if we ask again and again and again, the answer will come to us, and we will choose the right road.

Gandhi said, "Religions are different roads converging upon the same point. What does it matter that we take different roads as long as we reach the same goal?" And we are all struggling along the rocky, thorny road of the desert to reach God.

God, unlike some organized religions, does not discriminate. As long as you reach out to Her, She will go the better part of the way to meet you. There are an infinite number of roads to reach God. People can come to God through alcoholism, they can come to God through Zen Buddhism, as I did, and they can come to God through the multiple "New Thought" Christian churches even though they are distinctly heretical. For

161

all I know, they can come to God through Shirley MacLaine. People are at various stages of readiness, and when they're ready, virtually anything can speak to them.

A minister was shaking hands with the congregation of his Protestant church after the service, and at the end of the line there was a man whom he had seen only occasionally in church. The man came up and said, "Reverend, Reverend, what you said today in your sermon was exactly what I needed to hear. Thank you very, very much. It was so helpful to me. It revolutionized my life. Thank you, thank you."

The minister, quite pleased, said, "I'm glad I said something that was helpful to you, but I'm curious—what in particular was it?"

And the man answered, "Well, you may remember, you began your sermon by saying that you wanted to talk to us about two things this morning, and then in the middle you said, 'That completes this *first part* of what I wanted to tell you and now it's time I moved on to the *second part* of my sermon.' And at that moment I realized I had come to the end of the first part of my life, and it was high time that I got on to the second part. Thank you, Reverend, thank you, very much. "

MY ROAD TO GOD

I came to God through Zen Buddhism, but that was just the first stretch of the road. The road I have chosen for myself, after twenty years of dabbling with Zen, is Christianity. But I doubt that I could have made that choice without Zen. To accept Christianity one must be prepared to accept paradox, and Zen Buddhism—which a lot of people say shouldn't even be considered a religion but a philosophy—is the ideal training school for paradox. Without that training, I don't think there is any way I could have been prepared to swallow the literally God-awful paradoxes of Christian doctrine.

I became a Christian several years after *The Road Less Traveled* was published—and remember, the very first sentence in that book is the great Buddhist truth "Life is difficult"—although subconsciously I had been tending in that direction for quite some time, and *The Road Less Traveled* is full of Christian concepts. An important man said to me, "Scotty, it was so clever of you the way you disguised your Christianity in *The Road Less Traveled* in order to get the Christian message across to people." And I replied honestly, "Well, I didn't disguise my Christianity. I wasn't a Christian."

The Road Less Traveled can be looked at as very much a statement of where I was at that time in my journey. And in some ways I have come a great distance since then, and in some ways I have come a very short way. Much of what I have done since it was published has been a kind of working out of concepts that are in that book.

One of the inner events of my journey occurred around age thirty when I read C. S. Lewis's *The Screwtape Letters,* a novel composed of letters of advice from Screwtape, a senior demon, to his nephew, Wormwood, whose task is to undermine the spiritual life of a young man. At one point, Screwtape advises Wormwood to make sure that the man, now a young Christian due to their combined bungling, "regards his time as his time." This sentence, at first, made no sense to me. I read it three times. I wondered whether there might not be some typographical error. How else could anybody think of his time except as his own? Then it dawned on me that the possibility existed of my time belonging to a power higher than myself. For a good while it was a most discomfiting notion, and still today I am continuing to learn to submit my time to God's ownership. Submission is always a matter of degree, but it is teachable, just as C. S. Lewis taught it to me. It wasn't until a dozen years later, however, that I actually submitted to being baptized a Christian.

One of the reasons I very gradually gravitated toward Christianity is that I came to believe that Christian doctrine has the most correct understanding of the nature of sin. It is a paradoxical, multidimensional understanding, and the first side of the paradox is that Christianity holds that we are all sinners. We cannot not sin. There are a number of possible definitions of sin, but the most common is simply missing the mark, failing to hit the bull's-eye every time. And there's no way we can hit the bull's-eye every time. Sometimes we're going to be just a little careless. No matter how good we are, sometimes we're going to be a little tired or overconfident and not exert or extend ourselves quite enough. We cannot hit the bull's-eye every time; we cannot be perfect.

Christianity allows for that. In fact, the one prerequisite for membership in the true Christian church is that you be a sinner. If you do not think you are a sinner, you are not a candidate for the church. But the other side of the paradox is that Christianity holds that if you confess or acknowledge your sin with contrition, then it is wiped out. The word ''contrition'' is very important here, and what is required is feeling bad, suffering over what you have done. If you acknowledge your sin with contrition, then the slate is wiped clean. It is as if the sin never existed. You can start over again, fresh and clean every time.

There is a very sweet story about this concept. A little Filipino girl said she talked to Jesus, and people in her village began to get excited about that. Then word got around to some of the neighboring villages, and other people began to get excited about it. Finally, word reached the bishop's palace in Manila, and the bishop became somewhat concerned, because, after all, you can't have any unauthorized saints walking around in the Catholic church. So he appointed a monsignor to investigate this case.

The little girl was brought to the bishop's palace for a series of psychotheological diagnostic interviews. At the end of the third interview, the monsignor threw up his hands and said, "I just don't know, I don't know what to make of this. I don't know whether you're for real or not. But there is one acid test. The next time you talk to Jesus, I want you to ask Him what I confessed to at my last confession. Would you do that?" The little girl said she would. She went away and came back for her interview the next week, and with barely disguised eagerness the monsignor asked, "So, my dear, did you talk to Jesus again this past week?"

She said, "Yes, Father, I did."

"And when you talked to Jesus this past week, did you remember to ask Him what I confessed to at my last confession?"

"Yes, Father, I did."

"Well? When you asked Jesus what I confessed to at my last confession, what did Jesus say?"

And the little girl answered, "Jesus said, 'I've forgotten.' "

There are two possible interpretations to this story. One is that that girl was one smart little psychopath. But the more likely is that she really did talk to Jesus, because what she was expressing is pure, thoroughbred Christian doctrine. Once our sins are confessed with contrition, they are forgotten: they no longer exist in the mind of God.

THE REALITY OF JESUS

When people ask me whether I've been "born again," I say, "Well, maybe so. But if so, it was a very prolonged labor and difficult delivery." There were all kinds of milestones on that journey, but perhaps the most important was reading the Gospels for the first time at the age of forty. It was after I had written the first draft of *The Road Less Traveled*. I'm one of those people who tend to do their writing first and their research afterwards, so having quoted Jesus a couple of times, it seemed incumbent upon me to check out the references.

It was a very graceful time for me to come to the Gospels. Had you asked me a dozen years before whether Jesus was real, I would have said that there was more than enough evidence to indicate there was a historical Jesus, obviously a pretty wise chap who was executed in the manner of the day for speaking out a bit too much, and then, for some reason or another, people began to build a religion around him. That's what I would have replied, and I would have left His reality at that. I knew, you see, that the Gospel writers were not contemporaries of Jesus, that they were writing thirty or more years after His death, that what they wrote were obviously second- or third- or even fourth-hand accounts, and with my education in this age of enlightenment, I simply assumed that they were all into PR and embellishment.

166

But when I did finally come to read the Gospels, I did so with a dozen years of experience of trying in my own small way to be a teacher or healer, so I knew a little something about teaching and healing and what it's like to be a teacher and healer. With this experiential knowledge under my belt, I was absolutely thunderstruck by the extraordinary reality of the man I found in the Gospels. I discovered a man who was almost continually frustrated. His frustration leaps out of virtually every page: "What do I have to say to you? How many times do I have to say it? What do I have to do to get through to you?" I also discovered a man who was frequently sad and sometimes depressed, frequently anxious and scared. A man who was prejudiced on one occasion, although He was able to overcome that prejudice and transcend it in healing love. A man who was terribly, terribly lonely, yet often desperately needed to be alone. I discovered a man so incredibly real that no one could have made Him up.

It occurred to me then that if the Gospel writers had been into PR and embellishment, as I had assumed, they would have created the kind of Jesus three quarters of Christians still seem to be trying to create—what Lily refers to as "the wimpy Jesus." He is portrayed with a sweet, unending smile on His face, patting little children on the head, just strolling the earth with this unflappable, unshakable equanimity, because with His mellow-yellow Christ consciousness, He's got peace of mind. But the Jesus of the Gospels—who some suggest is the best-kept secret of Christianity—did not have much "peace of mind," as we ordinarily think of peace of mind in the world's terms, and insofar as we can be His followers, perhaps we won't either. Perhaps that's not the point.

So that's when I began to suspect that, rather than being public relations specialists, the Gospel writers were accurate reporters, generally going to great pains to record as accurately as possible the events and sayings in the life of a man they themselves hardly began to understand, but in whom they knew that Heaven and earth had met. And that's when I began to fall in love with Jesus.

It is as if most Christians haven't read the Gospels, and most Christian clergy are not even able to preach the real truth of the Gospels, because if they did, their congregations would flee out the door.

I don't want to imply that the Gospels are totally accurate. Some things obviously seem to have been added. Others seem to me to be obviously missing. Jesus' sense of humor, for instance, and His sexuality. The latter may have been left out on purpose because Jesus' sexuality seems to me rather ambiguous. He appears to have been very fond of Mary Magdalene, who might have been a prostitute, and He is frequently pictured in an intimate pose with the Apostle John, who is referred to as ''the one whom Jesus loved.'' I believe that Jesus was an androgynous figure; that is, not without sex, or unisexed, but whole. What does survive, however, shows Jesus to be really human, and a divine genius.

THE GENIUS OF JESUS

Lily and I used to belong to a little country club on the coast of Maine where we went every year or so for a few days in the summer. We were there just as *The Road Less Traveled* was being published, and in my narcissism I took pains to let it drop within the first twenty-four hours at the club that I was having a book published—that I was not only a psychiatrist but also an author. Shortly, I came to regret my narcissism, because the second night we were there, one of the other guests, who was quite a well-known litigation lawyer, approached me at cocktail hour and said, ''I hear you've written a book. What's it about?''

I answered, ''Well, it's a kind of integration of psychology and religion.''

''Fine, fine, but what does it say?'' he asked, with some of the abrasiveness that makes such specialists so good at their work.

''It says a whole bunch of things, and I'm not sure you want to sit here for an hour while I try to tell you all the things it says,'' I lamely replied.

He said, ''You're right, I don't. I want you to tell me in one or two succinct sentences what it says.''

And I said, ''Well, if I could do that, I wouldn't have had to write a book.''

''Nonsense,'' he persisted. ''We've got an expression in the law that anything worth saying can be said well in one or two succinct sentences.''

The best I could do was to comment, ''I guess that you'd really not find it worth hearing, then,'' and awkwardly slink away.

One example of the genius of Jesus was that when confronted with this same type of situation, He handled himself infinitely more gracefully. He was in some equivalent of a ''happy hour'' when out of the small crowd there stepped forth—you guessed it—a lawyer. The man said to him in effect, ''Well now, come on, Jesus, what is it that You are trying to say? I don't want a whole sermon on the mount or anything like that. Just tell me what Your message is in one or two succinct sentences. What are You trying to say?'' And Jesus obliged him: two sentences so succinct they can be rolled into one. Jesus said, ''Love the Lord your God with all your heart, and with all your soul and with all your might. And love your neighbor as yourself.''

That is a statement of what a Christian is—or should be. Unfortunately, most people don't understand the passion behind those words. To love God with all your heart and soul and might is to abandon yourself to Him. Abandoning yourself to God is a long and tough process, and I have come to discover many years after I became a Christian that I have not yet completed it.

After I had read the Gospels and *The Road Less Traveled* had been accepted for publication, I decided I deserved a vacation. I didn't want to do anything with the family, but I didn't want to travel alone and just sit on the beach someplace. Then I got this crazy idea to go on a retreat—that would be something different! So I went off for two weeks to a convent.

I had a number of agendas for this retreat. One was to try to stop smoking, which I succeeded in doing for that time alone. But my largest agenda item was to decide what to do if by some dim chance *The Road Less Traveled* made me famous. If that happened, should I give up my privacy and go out on the lecture circuit, or should I retire into the woods like J. D. Salinger and immediately get an unlisted phone number? I didn't know which way I wanted to go. And I didn't know which way God wanted me to go. So, at the top of my agenda was the hope that in the quietness of the retreat and the holiness of the atmosphere, I might get a revelation from God about how I should deal with this dilemma.

170

I thought I would do my best to help God out by paying attention to my dreams, since I believe that dreams can serve a certain revelatory function. So I started writing down my dreams, but they were mostly very simple images of bridges or gates, and they didn't tell me anything I didn't already know—namely, that I was at a point of transition in my life.

But I had one dream that was far more complex. In this dream, I was an onlooker in a distinctly middle-class home. In this home there was a seventeen-year-old boy who was the kind of son that every mother and father would love to have. He was president of the senior class in high school, he was going to be valedictorian at graduation time, he was captain of the high school football team, he was good-looking, he worked hard after school at a part-time job, and if all that wasn't enough, he had a girlfriend who was sweet and demure. Moreover, the boy had his driver's license, and was an unusually responsible, mature driver for his age. Only his father wouldn't let him drive. Instead, the father insisted on driving this boy wherever he had to go—football practice, job, dates, proms. And to add insult to injury, the father insisted that the boy pay him five dollars a week out of his hard-earned after-school earnings for the privilege of being driven around, which he was quite capable of doing himself. I awoke from this dream with a sense of absolute fury and outrage at what an autocratic creep the father was.

I didn't know what to make of the dream. It didn't seem to make any sense at all. But three days after I had written it down, when I was rereading what I had written, I noticed that I had capitalized the F in "Father." So I said to myself, "You don't happen to suppose that the father in this dream is God the Father, do you? And if that's the case, you don't suppose that you might be that seventeen-year-old boy?" And then I finally realized that I had gotten a revelation. God was saying to me, "Hey, Scotty, you just pay your dues and leave the driving to me."

It is interesting that I had always thought of God as being the ultimate good guy. Yet in my dream I had cast Him in the role of autocratic, overcontrolling villain, or at least I was responding to Him as such with fury and outrage and hatred. The problem, of course, was that this wasn't the revelation I had hoped for. It wasn't what I wanted to hear. I wanted some little bit of advice from God such as one might get from his agent or accountant, which I would be free to accept or reject. I didn't want a big revelation, particularly not one where God said, "I'm going to do the driving after this."

Sixteen years later I'm still trying to live up to this revelation, to abandon myself to God by learning the surrender that welcomes His or Her being in the driver's seat of my still adolescent life.

BAPTISM AS DEATH

Another thing that happened on that two-week retreat was that I began to toy with the notion of becoming a Christian. It was not a very pleasant notion. To act on it, I felt, would require a kind of death on several levels. For one, there was this old business of me being in the driver's seat of *my* time. It seemed to me that if I were to become a Christian my time would no longer belong to me, that it would have to belong to Christ/God and to the mystical "Body of Christ." My ownership of my time would have to die, and that very much felt like having to die myself.

No one likes to die, and so I dragged my feet as long as I could. I used every rationalization in the book to avoid being baptized. The best was that I couldn't decide whether I wanted to be baptized as an Eastern Orthodox, or Roman Catholic, or Episcopalian, or Presbyterian or Lutheran or Methodist or Baptist. Since this complex, intellectual denominational decision was obviously going to take at least thirty years of research, I didn't have to get on with it. But then it hit me that I didn't have to choose a denomination, that, in fact, baptism is not a denominational celebration. So when I was finally drowned March 9, 1980, it was by a North Carolina Methodist minister at the chapel of a New York Episcopal convent in a deliberately nondenominational party. And I have very jealously guarded my nondenominational status ever since. For one thing, it is good for business. But the more compelling reason is that, on a certain deep level, I don't believe in denominations. I do believe there should be different flavors of worship for different folk, but the idea of one denomination denying Communion to another—or to any individual at all—is anathema to me. As far as I am concerned, I feel free to walk into a Christian church of whatever denomination because I belong there.

SINS OF THE CHURCH

I would not have become a Christian or have been baptized at the age of forty-three if I thought that Christianity was a second-best religion, or that one religion was just as good as another. On the intellectual level, the reason I became a Christian is that I gradually came to believe that, on the whole, Christian doctrine approaches the reality of God and reality in general more closely than the other great religions. This doesn't mean that there isn't a great deal to be learned from the other religions. There's an enormous amount to be learned, and it is the responsibility of any educated Christian to garner as much of the wisdom of other religious traditions as she or he possibly can.

Perhaps the greatest sin of the Christian church has been that particular brand of arrogance, or narcissism, that impels so many Christians to feel they have got God all sewn up and put in their back pocket. Those who think that they've got the whole truth and nothing but the truth, and that those other poor slobs who believe differently are necessarily not saved, as far as I'm concerned have a very small God. They don't realize the truth that God is bigger than their own theology. As I've said, God is not ours to possess, but we are His or Hers to be possessed by. And there is nothing that does more than this narrow-minded narcissism to de-evangelize Christianity.

When I became a Christian, I knew that in identifying myself as such I would have to take upon myself, in one way or another, the burden of the sins of the Christian church, of which arrogance is only one. Another of the burdens of those sins is having to atone for such atrocities as the virulent anti-Semitism of the church throughout the ages and more recently the church's failure to stop the Holocaust. I am convinced that had the Christian churches—as they should have—declared Nazism to be incompatible with Christianity, labeled it worse than heresy and threatened all Nazis with excommunication, the course of history would have been very different.

Still another one of the burdens of those sins is to be misunderstood. As soon as I mention Jesus or Christianity, many people take offense either because they are of a different religion or because of the experience they have had with the hypocrisy of the church. One of those people was my own wife, who, as the daughter of a Chinese Conservative Baptist minister, was raised in a home where faith and love were preached, but where fear and hate were the order of the day. So there I was, beginning to get excited about all these "new" concepts which I associated with positive meanings, and to Lily they represented red flags of hypocrisy. It was a very painful time for us until gradually I learned to become much less "preachy" and she learned that there are different levels of Christianity, as in all religions, and I wasn't on the same level that her parents had been.

So I knew full well before I was baptized that if I spoke out about my beliefs, there were many who would dislike me and tune me out by virtue of their often understandable prejudice. But one of the things that Jesus taught is that life is not a popularity contest. Still, another way in which my baptism was a death for me was the very act of publicly declaring myself a Christian and thereby assuming this small burden of prejudice.

In bearing it I have found some consolation in a magazine originally called *The Wittenberg Door* and now renamed simply *The Door*. It is a magazine of Christian humor—which some might think is a contradiction in terms. It's put out by a group of evangelicals diction in terms. It's put out by a group of evangelicals who are deeply offended by the sins of the church and its oh-so-common blasphemy and distortion of decent evangelism. They deal with that by poking fun at it. Each issue features the "Green Weenie Award" given to the most tasteless example of Christianity. One month it was the Bible Belt—a belt made out of snakeskin that had a miniature Bible attached to it.

They feature songs like:

Drop kick me Jesus
through the goal posts of life,
Straight over, end over end,
through those righteous uprights.

So I am tuned out by many Stage Two Christians, some of whom have even picketed my lectures, calling me "the anti-Christ." I am also tuned out by a few New Agers as being too conservative. I never thought I would be a middle-of-the-road anything, and here I've found myself a middle-of-the-road Christian. And as bad as that might sound, it is good, I've decided. It is not fence-sitting. It is a path of tension. An important doctrine of Buddhism is called the Middle Path, which stands for the embracing of opposites. Buddha himself, after following two paths of extremes—one of study and one of asceticism—chose the middle path. It was after he had almost starved himself to death that he sat under the tree and became enlightened. The Chinese like to portray him as fat, because fatness means prosperity in the Chinese culture. Occasionally you might run across a skinny, wasted Buddha, but generally he is depicted as neither fat nor skinny, but as middle-of-the-road.

LIFE AFTER DEATH

While I continue to make use of what I have learned from Buddhism, there are aspects of Buddhism—like reincarnation—that I am an agnostic about. That means I don't disbelieve it and I don't believe it; I just don't know.

On the one hand, there is a psychiatrist, Dr. Ian Stevenson, who has been investigating reincarnation in his spare time for years. The last time I heard about his work, which was a decade or so ago, he completely debunked hypnotic regression to past lives, but had discovered some seven cases which he simply could not explain except through the concept of reincarnation. If someone as rigorous as Dr. Stevenson believes in reincarnation, then it is something I have to take seriously. On the other hand, I am extremely leery of any doctrine that can be used to explain everything. And the idea of reincarnation can be used—or misused—to explain everything.

William James in his *Varieties of Religious Experience* brought up the notion of "old souls," which I do not discount. He said that there are certain people who seem to be born with the knowledge to live life as if they had lived before. I have known children who seem to be capable of extraordinary flashes of wisdom, and I wrote my children's book, *The Friendly Snowflake,* "for young people with old souls and older people with young souls."

While open to the possibility of reincarnation, I perhaps would be more passionate about it were there not an alternative way of dealing with the issue, which has come to appeal to me much more deeply—namely, the traditional Christian belief in life after death with its concepts of Heaven, Hell, and Purgatory. Although Purgatory is primarily a Roman Catholic notion, the psychiatrist in me takes to it with ease. I imagine Purgatory as a very elegant, well-appointed psychiatric hospital with the most modern and highly developed techniques for making learning as gentle and painless as possible under divine supervision.

On the other hand, I find distasteful the traditional idea of Christianity which preaches the resurrection of the body. Frankly, I see my body as more of a limitation than a virtue, and I will be glad to be free of it rather than having to continue to cart it around. I prefer to believe that souls can exist independently from bodies. I think it is possible for souls to exist independently of bodies and even to be developed independently of bodies. Certainly all the literature describing near-death experiences tends to support this view.

HELL

My view of Hell is also not so traditionally Christian, although I am mainly indebted for it to C. S. Lewis, the greatest Christian writer of this century. His novel *The Great Divorce* is a story about a group of people in Hell—which he depicts as a miserable, gray British Midlands city—who manage to get on a bus which takes them to Heaven. Heaven is very bright and cheerful, a delightful place. They are greeted with great hospitality and warmth by their friends and relatives. But by the end of the day, all except one of the people have gotten back onto the bus, and it is still left a bit unclear about that one. All but one choose to go back to Hell!

Why? Lewis uses many examples. Taking the liberty

of condensing some of them in a composite, I cite this as typical of what happens to all of them. Let's say one of the people on the bus is a man who is welcomed by his nephew. He is surprised to find his nephew in Heaven, because he thought the young man had never amounted to much on earth. But the nephew is very welcoming and Heaven is bright and cheerful. The man says, "This seems a nice enough sort of place and I might want to stay here. Now, as you know, I was a professor of history at Columbia University. Do you have universities here?"

The nephew says, "Yes, Uncle, of course."

"I assume that I would get tenure."

"But of course you'd get tenure. Everybody in Heaven has tenure."

The uncle is astonished. "How is it possible for everyone to get tenure? Don't you distinguish between the competent and the incompetent?"

The nephew says, "Everybody is competent here, Uncle."

That doesn't sit well with the uncle, but he continues to interrogate his nephew. "As you know, I was chairman of the department, and I assume I would be chairman here."

"I'm sorry, but we don't have chairmen. It doesn't work that way. Everyone is responsible, so we work by consensus and just don't seem to need chairpeople anymore."

That's when the uncle sputters, "If you think I am going to join some kind of half-baked organization that doesn't distinguish between the competent and the riff-raff, you've got another think coming." So he boards the bus and goes back to Hell.

179

My vision of Hell is distinctly like that of Lewis. The gates of Hell are wide open. People can walk right out of Hell, and the reason they are in Hell is that they choose not to. I know that is not traditionally Christian, but there are many ways that I deviate from traditional Christianity. I simply cannot accept the view of Hell in which God punishes people without hope and destroys souls without a chance for redemption. He/ She wouldn't go to the trouble of creating souls, with all their complexity, just to fry them in the end.

GOD AS AN EFFICIENCY EXPERT

People often ask me to name the most influential book I've ever read, and I wish I could say that it was Plato or Aristotle or Thomas Aquinas. But, in fact, the book that has perhaps had the greatest influence on me was *Cheaper by the Dozen* by Frank Gilbreth, which I ran across when I was about ten or eleven. It is the true story of a couple who have twelve children, and because the parents are, in fact, efficiency experts, they run their large family with extreme efficiency. It was the first time I had ever encountered the concept of an efficiency expert, and I thought, "Wow, that would be a neat thing to become when I grow up!" In some ways I like to think that is what I have become—as a psychotherapist trying to help people live their lives more efficiently, and then as a lecturer and writer trying to help them live their lives more efficiently, and very much in my work with community trying to help groups behave more efficiently.

As an efficiency expert—if I am that—I admire other people who are good at it, and so I am in awe of

God's efficiency. For example, in 1982, I took a much reduced fee to do a lecture and workshop at a Mormon conference in Salt Lake City because I thought it would be a marvelous opportunity to learn more about Mormonism. At the last moment, I asked our older daughter, who was twenty then, whether she would like to go along with me to Salt Lake City, and she said she would. It proved to be a very healing time in our relationship. We made several good friends out there, I got all that I had hoped in terms of learning about Mormonism, and my engagement was very successful.

About three days after I returned to Connecticut, I got a phone call from a woman who wanted an appointment. She came in a few days later, and it turned out that she was a Mormon. She told me that she had been very nurtured in some ways by the Mormon church, but felt very oppressed by it in other ways, and was conflicted by that. I don't think there was any way I could have understood her as deeply as I did, nor empathized with her dilemmas, had I not just been to that conference. Now, there are not many Mormons in rural northwestern Connecticut, and it so happens that in ten years of busy practice there, this was the first such patient who had ever crossed my threshold, and I asked, ''God, did You send me out to Salt Lake City simply to prepare me to work with this woman?'' Then I thought of all the other beneficial things that had been accomplished on that trip, and the efficiency of God amazed me. Not a wasted motion!

Lily and I have a beautiful flower garden which we have relished tending over the years. Flower gardens do not just happen. To develop a really fine flower garden takes an enormous amount of money and time and love and care. It would be inconceivable for me to take a bulldozer or a flamethrower and just devastate the garden that we have poured so much energy and care into. That's my feeling about life after death. Knowing God's efficiency, it makes no sense to me that She/He should put so much energy into developing souls just to obliterate them, to waste them. There must be something more.

HEAVEN

I have spoken about Hell and Purgatory. What about Heaven?

Some people are referring to me these days as a "lay theologian," by which I think they mean someone who talks about God but hasn't read anything. But one thing that real theologians are now universally well agreed upon is that God loves variety. In variety, She/He delights. Sit in a meadow on a lazy summer afternoon and look about you. Without even moving, you will be able to see dozens of different species of plants. Hundreds of different kinds of insects will be buzzing around in the air. And if you had microscopic vision, you could look into the soil and see whole societies and cultures of viruses and bacteria intermingling. What variety!

Or look at the human race. Over the years I have come not only to be more and more impressed by the extraordinary variety of human beings but also to depend upon it. We are male and female, straight and gay, white, yellow, red, and black, old and young, Jewish and Christian and Muslim and Hindu, and what a dreary world it would be if we were all middle-aged Episcopalians.

Because God so loves variety, the one thing I can

surmise with any assurance about Heaven is that it does not conform to the stereotypical notion of identical cherubs with standard-issue halos and harps sitting around on fluffy clouds. Perhaps the most commonly quoted sentence at funerals is: "In my Father's house there are many mansions." When I was a child, I used to think that this was simply an expression of the magnificence of size alone. I thought it to mean that God's house—or Heaven—was so magnificently huge that it could contain within it a large number of smaller mansions. But now I interpret it as a statement of variety, and I suspect that when we get to Heaven, we will indeed find many mansions there, some of which will be Colonials, some will be ranch-type, some stucco, and some wood, some will have swimming pools, some will be built on cliffs and others in valleys. In my Father's house there will be many mansions!

Beyond this, I don't know. All this business of Heaven, Hell, and Purgatory is what is called "speculative theology." The best we can do is to speculate. We won't know until we have been freed from our bodies by death.

Speaking of knowing, my primary identity—before that of a religious person—is that of a scientist. We scientists are what are called empiricists. Empiricism holds that the best—not the only, but the best—route to knowledge is through experience. So what do we scientists do but conduct experiments—or controlled experiences—from which we can learn and eventually know? Thus it has been through the experiences of my life—my experiences of grace—that I have come to what little knowledge I have about God.

In this regard, I am very much like Carl Jung, another scientist. Toward the end of his life he submitted himself to a film interview. After many rather prosaic questions, the interviewer finally said, "Dr. Jung, a lot of your writing has a religious flavor. Do you believe in God?"

Old Jung puffed on his pipe. "Believe in God?" he mused out loud. "Well, we use the word 'believe' when we think that something is true but we don't yet have a substantial body of evidence to support it. No. I don't believe in God. I *know* there's a God."

CHAPTER TEN

Matter and Spirit

T here is a hunger these days, a gnawing dissatisfaction with the answers provided by materialism and scientific progress, a craving for an inner life . . . Increasingly, Americans are looking for solutions that speak to the spirit as well as the psyche.

These lofty words did not come from the latest inspirational best-seller. They came from a December 7, 1992, issue of *U.S. News & World Report.* The magazine devoted five of its pages to trying to explain why Carl Jung has suddenly become so appealing, more than thirty years after his death, and concluded that Jung provides a perfect marriage between psychology and spirituality, between religion and science.

The Road Less Traveled was once described as ''Jung translated for the masses,'' and its popularity obviously has a great deal to do with the fact that it was published at the right time, just when this ''gnawing dissatisfaction'' was beginning to be felt. Its popularity surprised me, because I wasn't saying anything new. I was repeating things that Carl Jung and William James and others had said long before me. Then I realized that although I wasn't saying anything new, people had not listened before. Now they were ready to pay attention. I realized that people had changed.

Soon after its publication, *The Road Less Traveled* seemed to have great appeal to people living in the Bible Belt, and at first the vast majority of requests for me to lecture came from that area. This was astonishing to me since I am not a fundamentalist. But then it dawned on me that the people who wanted to hear me speak might live in the Bible Belt but did not share the fundamentalist mentality. There were a great many people out there who had preserved their passion for God and spirituality but were fed up to the gills with a simplistic black-and-white religious faith that claims to have all the answers and doesn't deal with mystery. They were yearning for some fresh air. They needed some way to bridge the gulf between a purely materialistic science and a rigid, doctrinaire theology.

To understand why that gulf existed, we have to go back in time before there was such a thing as psychology. We need to examine the history of the relationship between religion and science.

Some twenty-five hundred years ago, the original relationship between religion and science was one of integration. And this integration had a name—philosophy. So early philosophers like Plato and Aristotle, and later ones like Thomas Aquinas, were men of scientific bent. They thought in terms of evidence and they questioned premises, but they also were totally convinced that God was an essential reality.

But in the sixteenth century things began to go sour, and they hit bottom in 1633 when Galileo was summoned before the Inquisition. The results of that event were decidedly unpleasant. They were unpleasant for

Galileo, who was forced to recant his beliefs in Copernican theory—that the planets revolve around the sun—and then was placed under house arrest for the remainder of his life. However, in short order, things got even more unpleasant for the church.

To describe what happened next, let me indulge in a fantasy. Imagine that the year is 1705 and we are in London, England, privileged to be witnesses to a secret meeting in the private offices of Queen Anne herself. To this meeting, traveling in secret all the way from Rome, has come Pope Clement XI. And responding to a summons from his queen has come, from his laboratories at the Royal Society of London for Improving Natural Knowledge, none other than Isaac Newton.

The Queen begins the meeting by saying: ''As you know, I have God-given responsibility for the political order and stability of our civilization. I am grateful to His Holiness for recently sending me a secret message which suggested an action that might be taken to help me fulfill, by God's grace, those responsibilities. Since it was at your initiation that this meeting came to pass, Your Holiness, perhaps you would be so kind as to convey to Mr. Newton the sense of your message. ''

''Thank you, Your Majesty,'' says the Pope. ''As you know, Mr. Newton, the Galileo affair has been of considerable embarrassment to the church for some years now. All I did was to propose to your queen that it is high time that there should be some healing in the conflict between science and religion. ''

''Such would certainly be in the best interest of the state,'' says the Queen.

Newton is quick to respond that the means and aims of science as they have developed over the past century have become quite different from those of religion. "The age of the armchair philosopher is past," he says. "I do not see how we can turn back the clock or that we should attempt to do so."

"Oh, I quite agree, Mr. Newton," says the Pope. "A true reunification is not possible, but surely there could be some reconciliation at least, a rapprochement of sorts, between the scientific and the religious communities."

"But what do you want me to do?" asks Newton.

"A deal, Isaac," says the Queen. "The time has come to make a deal."

"An agreement, Mr. Newton," says the Pope. "As the representative of the Holy See, I am empowered to make an agreement whereby the church would no longer harass any genuine member of the scientific establishment, as long as the scientific establishment agrees, in turn, to keep its scientific nose out of religious matters."

"What we are proposing, Isaac," says the Queen, "is a mutual respect for each other's territories, through a stable balance of power and a cooperative relationship in which everyone's back can be scratched. This is an accord with already existing boundaries. The aim of your society—which, I might add, currently thrives under my auspices and protection—is, as its title suggests, to improve natural knowledge. Now, natural knowledge is quite different from supernatural knowledge, which I'm sure you will agree is quite properly the province of the church."

"Just as politics is quite properly the domain of the politician," says the Pope. "Surely the scientific quest for natural knowledge should not be sullied by the vagaries of vulgar politics. Should science stand above political concerns as well as aside from religious matters, I can even foresee the possibility of support for science in the form of government subsidies for scientific departments within the universities as well as for the increasingly complex equipment coming to be required for scientific investigation.''

"Quite possibly," says the Queen. "Should you be willing to support the idea of pure science along the lines we have been considering, Isaac, well then, the church would be able to create an image of the pure scientist as a public hero.''

"Which would surely pave the way," says the Pope, "for public tax moneys to be made available for scientific investigation, properly restricted to natural phenomena.''

Newton sits for a lengthy moment in obviously thoughtful silence. Finally he says, "Well, the advantages of the arrangement do seem rather compelling.''

The Queen smiles. "As president of the Royal Society, Isaac, you are the most influential scientist in Christendom. If you can support the development of the ideal of pure science we have been describing, I have no doubt that a giant step will have been taken to ensure the stability of Christian civilization for centuries to come. But of course, it all must be done rather quietly. This is a subtle sort of business. It is a matter of vision. I see no need for us to mention this meeting to anyone. It should all be done without any fanfare. I know that I can count on your cooperation.''

"I'll see what I can do, Your Majesty," says Newton.

"Oh, thank you, Isaac," says the Queen. "And by the way, since I know that you can keep secrets, I see no harm in telling you now that I have been seriously considering you for knighthood before the year is out.''

THE UNWRITTEN CONTRACT

So ends my fantasy. Of course, no such meeting took place. But just such an unwritten social contract dividing up the territory between government, science, and religion was developed toward the end of the seventeenth and the beginning of the eighteenth centuries. It was not consciously developed. It was an almost unconscious response to the needs of the day. Nonetheless, this unwritten social contract has done more than anything else to determine the nature of our science and our religion ever since.

Indeed, it might be looked upon as one of the great intellectual happenings of humankind. All manner of good came from it: the Inquisition faded away, religious folk stopped burning witches, the coffers of the church remained full for several centuries, slavery was abolished, democracy was established without anarchy, and, perhaps because it did restrict itself to natural phenomena, science thrived, giving birth to a technological revolution beyond anybody's wildest expectations, even to the point of paving the way for the development of a planetary culture.

The problem is that this unwritten social contract no longer works. Indeed, at this point in time, it is becoming downright diabolic. You may know that the word *diabolic* comes from the Greek *diaballein*, which means "to throw apart or to separate, to compartmentalize." It is the opposite of *symbolic*, which comes from the word *symballein*, meaning "to throw together, to unify." This unwritten social contract is tearing us apart.

THE EVIL OF COMPARTMENTALIZATION

When I was working for the armed services in 1970-71, I used to wander the halls of the Pentagon, talking to people about the Vietnam War. I could get away with this kind of thing because I was in uniform. I would go to people and ask about the war, and they would say, "Well, yes, Dr. Peck, we understand your concerns. Yes, we do. But you see, we're the ordnance branch here, and we are only responsible for seeing to it that the napalm is manufactured and sent to Vietnam on time. We really don't have anything to do with the war. The war is the responsibility of the policy branch. Go down the hall and talk to the people in policy."

So I would go down the hall and talk to people in policy, and they would say, "Yes, Dr. Peck, we understand your concerns. Yes, we do. But here in the policy branch, we simply execute policy, we don't really make policy. Policy is made at the White House." Thus, it appeared that the whole Pentagon had absolutely nothing to do with the Vietnam War.

This same kind of compartmentalization can happen in any large organization. It can happen in businesses and in other areas of government, it can happen in hospitals and universities, it can happen in churches. When any institution becomes so large and compartmentalized, with departments and subdepartments, then the conscience of the institution will often become so fragmented and diluted as to be virtually nonexistent, and the organization becomes inherently evil.

The same kind of compartmentalization can occur within individuals as well. Human beings have a remarkable capacity to take things that are related to each other and stick them in separate airtight compartments so they don't rub up against each other and cause them much pain. We're all familiar with the man who goes to church on Sunday morning, believing that he loves God and God's creation and his fellow human beings, but who, on Monday morning, has no trouble with his company's policy of dumping toxic wastes in the local stream. He can do this because he has religion in one compartment and his business in another. He is what we have come to know as a "Sunday morning Christian." It is a very comfortable way to operate, but integrity it is not.

The word *integrity* comes from the same root as *integrate*. It means to achieve wholeness, which is the opposite of compartmentalize. Compartmentalization is easy. Integrity is painful. But without it there can be no wholeness. Integrity requires that we be fully open to the conflicting forces and ideas and stresses in life.

ABORTION AND INTEGRITY

The issue of abortion is one such conflict. I've been torn apart trying to resolve this issue with integrity. It seems to me that arbitrarily assigning a moment to when life begins—whether in the first trimester or the second trimester—is just a way of evading the issue. Obviously life begins at conception, and obviously any interruption of that life involves the killing of a human being. I also believe that a simple policy of abortion on demand can tend to diminish what Albert Schweitzer called our "reverence for life."

On the other hand, there is the life of the woman to consider. And the father. And the society. The lives of many women would have been seriously damaged had they carried a child to term, even if they intended to give that child up for adoption—and not every child is adoptable. Or lives would have been damaged if they carried a child to term and then tried to parent it while not being capable of parenting a child. So I don't have the answer to abortion, except to say that any simplistic, one-dimensional answer like "Thou shall not abort" simply isn't going to cut it.

My rule of thumb whenever I am faced with a proposed social solution is to bear in mind the question "What is missing?" And if you ask what is missing in a law that proclaims "Thou shall not abort," the answer you get is responsibility. Responsibility is missing. The lawmakers take the responsibility away from the mother or parents of the unborn child by simply declaring: "You must bear that child." But where do they place that responsibility? The answer is nowhere. They certainly do not want the responsibility themselves for the child once it is born. Therefore, a law that proclaims "Thou shall not abort" is a law without compassion and integrity.

I actually look forward to the day when we might be able to say "Thou shall not abort" *with* compassion and integrity. But the only way we can do that is within community, where it becomes a community decision whether there should or shouldn't be an abortion. If there should, then the community takes upon itself some of the guilt around the decision. But if it decides that there shouldn't be an abortion, then the community assumes some responsibility for the financial and psychological welfare not only of that child but also of its parents. Of course, we don't even begin to have enough community in this country either to fit the bill or to foot the bill. Until such time as we do, a simplistic policy against abortion would be atavistic and would achieve nothing except to return us to where we were forty years ago when the poor had coat hangers and the rich their trips to Sweden.

So, if you want to think with integrity—as long as you're willing to bear the pain involved—all you need do is to remember to ask this single question: "What is missing?" But it is not always comfortable, because sooner or later you will come to the realization that, on a certain level, each of us needs to be responsible for *everything*.

WHAT IS MISSING?

I first learned to look for what is missing during the Korean War. I was fourteen years old then, and I used to enjoy running out every morning to get *The New York Times*. One day I'd read that thirty-seven MIGs were shot down—a great triumph for the American air force, which suffered no casualties whatsoever. The next day I would be happy again to read that forty-one MIGs were shot down, and all American planes returned to home base. And the next day forty-three MIGs were shot down, and only one American plane was lost. The next day, thirty-nine MIGs were shot down, and all American planes were safe, and then forty-three MIGs were shot down, and only one American plane was slightly damaged. While I grieved over the rare loss of a plane or pilot, I rejoiced at these statistics, which, the same *Times* explained, were the result of the superior manufacture of the American planes and the shoddy work of the Russian plane builders. The *Times* also said that our American pilots were much better trained than the poor starving Chinese or North Korean pilots who had inferior reflexes.

The same *New York Times* also referred to China and

Russia as underdeveloped countries. And year after year, as these statistics went on, I began to wonder how industrially underdeveloped countries could manufacture all those MIGs, shoddily made as they were, just to be shot down. After a while it dawned on me that something was missing. Ever since then I've never quite been able to believe everything I read in *The New York Times*.

I learned the lesson again in medical school when Lily and I read *Atlas Shrugged* by Ayn Rand, a book that so compellingly puts forth a philosophy of rugged individualism and unrestrained self-interest that I was tempted to convert to being a right-wing Republican. But something vaguely bothered me about it, and it wasn't until ten days or so after I finished reading it that I realized that in this panoramic novel of almost twelve hundred pages there are virtually no children. Children were missing. Of course, that's exactly where Rand's philosophy of unrestrained self-interest and rugged individualism begins to break down—with children and people in our society who need other people.

And all of these lessons came together in my psychiatry training when I learned that what the patient says is not as important as what the patient doesn't say. If you have patients who talk freely about the present and the future but never about the past, you can bet your bottom dollar that they have some problem, something that's unintegrated from their past. Or if they talk freely about the past and the future but not about the present, again the problem is most likely to be the present—often a problem with vulnerability and the ''here and now.'' Or if they talk about the past and the present but don't talk about the future, you can guess there's a problem with the future—a problem with hope or faith.

COMPARTMENTALIZATION IN PSYCHIATRY

When the patient's problem is one of hope and faith—and in many other circumstances—psychotherapy fails if it is compartmentalized rather than integrated, or if it does not deal with the question of values. When I was in psychiatric training, we were taught that, following the model of pure science, psychotherapy should be a value-free kind of endeavor. The therapist must stay clear of all issues involving values, and be careful not to impose his or her values upon a patient. To do so would be to step into the dreaded realm of counter-transference, and therapy would be contaminated and no longer pure.

My otherwise brilliant psychiatry residency chief lectured all of us students that a good therapist should, by the second or third session with a patient, tell him or her, ''I am not here to judge you.'' Having committed that to heart, when I began to see outpatients for lengthy psychotherapy I told the first dozen I saw that I was not there to judge them. It was a lot of nonsense. The reason that entering therapy is such a courageous act is precisely because patients know that nothing will be accomplished unless they submit themselves to judgment.

The fact of the matter is that there has never been such a thing as value-free psychotherapy. It's simply that psychotherapists have been unconscious of their own value system, and the predominant value system with which they've been operating is called secular humanism. It is a value system which puts the emphasis on earthly problems and dismisses otherworldly concerns. In many ways it is a very good value system, and many of those who attack it would be well advised to become more like the secular humanists whom they condemn.

Let me give you a couple of examples of the values of secular humanism. Freud, an atheist, defined mental health in terms of *lieben* and *arbeiten*, which mean "love" and "work." Loving well is a value of secular humanism, as is working productively. Another example: About fifteen years ago, I was seeing an extremely depressed woman, and talking with her was like pulling teeth. The first year of our work together, she would come in for her appointment and say, "Well, I'm more depressed this week." And I would ask, "Well, why do you think that is?" And she would immediately answer, "I don't know." Sometimes she would come in and say, "I'm less depressed this week." And I would inquire, "Well, why do you think that is?" And she would instantly reply, "I don't know."

Finally I said, "Listen, I've asked you to think about something, and you answer 'I don't know' in one thousandth of a millisecond. There's no way you could have done what I've asked you to do—namely, to think. Before we get any further, the first thing you're going to need to learn how to do is to think." Thinking is a value of secular humanism.

The value system of secular humanism is sufficient for the treatment of perhaps sixty percent of psychiatric patients. However, it is insufficient for the treatment of approximately forty percent. And that is why, for example, AA has been much more effective than psychiatry in treating alcoholics, who, generally speaking, fall into this forty percent. This is partly because, as we have discussed, AA addresses the spiritual needs of these people—something that traditional psychotherapy, with its secular humanist values, does not address.

Spiritual/religious ideas and concepts are necessary in the treatment of many people, and not only addicts and alcoholics. Those suffering from phobias are often another case in point. In my own practice, everyone who has come to me with a specific phobia about a certain street, or cats, or planes, has also turned out—as I got to know them better—not to be very keen on interstates, or dogs, or trains. And I would come to find out that, in fact, they were phobic about life. They had what I would call phobic personalities.

Over the years, in working with a few of these patients, I was struck by the fact that their views of the world had two significant features in common. One, they regarded the world as being a very dangerous place, and two, they felt themselves all alone in this dangerous world in which it was up to them to survive solely by their own wits. Feeling this way, they would tend, through their phobias, to limit the scope of their activity, to narrow the world down to a space over which they could have complete control and hence where they could feel safe.

About fifteen years ago, for example, I was working with a woman among whose many phobias was the fear of the water and of swimming. She had children who were five and seven—the swimming age—so this phobia bothered her especially. She was afraid to go swimming with them. After we had been working for about a year, she came in one day and told me what a wonderful weekend she had had, and that on Sunday she had gone to a pool party, where she had a grand time swimming around with the kids in the pool. Nothing of extraordinary psychodynamic significance had happened as far as I knew, so I scratched my head and I said, ''I thought you were phobic about swimming." And she said, "Well, I am, but I'm not phobic about swimming pools." That puzzled me. "What makes swimming pools different?" I asked. And she said, "Oh, in swimming pools, the water is clear." So I learned she wasn't phobic about swimming but just about lakes, rivers, and oceans, into which she could only go up to her ankles or knees. Beyond that she was unable to see her toes. And then God knows what might happen to them! She had lost control of her toes.

After a while I realized that there was no way to treat such people effectively without trying to *convert* them to a more benign worldview: a view of the world either as less dangerous than they thought or at least as a place in which they were not all alone, but had some kind of protection in the form of God's grace.

I believe that the *judicious* use of religious concepts can also enhance or speed up psychotherapy in many of the remaining cases that are susceptible to the traditional approach. Such concepts can be used both to confront and to console. For example, when people need to stop feeling sorry for themselves, I might remind them that Jesus taught us to carry our crosses joyfully. But others who are particularly conscientious may need permission to feel sorry for themselves every once in a while. To such a patient, I would say that while Jesus taught us to carry our crosses joyfully, He didn't expect us to carry them joyfully twenty-four hours a day. Anyone who can do that has got some kind of brain damage. "What was Jesus feeling when he climbed Mount Golgotha with three hundred pounds on his back?" I would ask them to imagine. He was feeling sorry for Himself. So I would point out to these patients that they're entitled to take five minutes twice a day to feel sorry for themselves.

Another example I have made frequent use of is that of Saint Thérèse of Lisieux, who said: "If you are willing to serenely bear the trial of being displeasing to yourself, then you will be for Jesus a pleasant place of shelter." If I was working with someone who was suffering from realistic guilt—let's say a Vietnam veteran having nightmares because he had killed innocent children in wartime—then I might say to him, "Let's celebrate the fact that you're going through this guilt and that you are truly displeased with yourself, because now you are for Jesus a pleasant place of shelter. ' And I could console him with that.

On the other hand, if I was working with a man who had a Christian identity but was not experiencing existential guilt—who was notably self-righteous and self-satisfied—I would likely confront him by asking, "Gee, what do you think Saint Thérèse meant by 'the trial of being displeasing to yourself'?"

These words from Saint Thérèse I have found particularly useful in understanding patients with depressive personalities, who are real experts at being displeasing to themselves. They would say to me, "Dr. Peck, I'm such a useless human being. I've never done anything worthwhile in my life. I know back in the service I was a three-star admiral, but that was just a fluke. I don't know why you'd want to see somebody like me. I'm no good to my wife, I'm no good to my children, I'm no good to anybody. Oh God, it must be hard for you to keep seeing a wretch like me week after week."

Saint Thérèse who died at the age of twenty-four, was a smart woman who chose her words carefully. Remember, she said, "If you are willing to *serenely* bear the trial of being displeasing to yourself . . .'' The problem with depressives is that they're not particularly serene about it. And indeed, such excessive breast-beating was labeled by the Catholic church centuries ago as the sin of ''excessive scrupulosity,'' and correctly diagnosed as a perverted form of the sin of pride. What these people are really saying is, ''I know God forgives me but I'll be the judge.'' If you scratch through their pseudo-humility, you frequently come to a core of arrogance and narcissism.

Many articles have appeared in professional journals recently about something called the cognitive theory of depression. Psychiatrists have figured out that depressed people do not cognate the same way as nondepressed people. By cognition they mean not just thought but all that goes into thinking, including perception. Specifically, depressed people selectively perceive the negative in the world, both inside and outside, and they fail to perceive the positive.

For many years Lily fought a heroic battle against depression, which she ultimately won, but before she won it, we used to go out in the backyard of our house on a May morning and I would look around and think to myself, ''Isn't it wonderful that spring is here and the grass is turning green and the trees are in bud, and how fortunate we are to live in this lovely old Colonial house! It needs some painting, but we'll get around to it next year and thank God we've got the money for it.'' But Lily would be standing next to me saying, ''When is Fritz going to come and mow the lawn? And look, somebody left the clippers out all night and look at this house—it's a mess.'' Two people standing within the same few square feet but perceiving totally different worlds.

So psychiatrists have figured out that in treating depressives it's often necessary to teach them how to cognate differently. To stop selectively perceiving the negative, these people need to be taught to perceive the positive. But the psychiatrists who are just now catching on to this might be a little bit embarrassed to realize that their new "cognitive therapy" is no different from Norman Vincent Peale's *The Power of Positive Thinking*, a book written decades ago. Actually, the most succinct words ever spoken about depression were spoken in the twelfth century by Jalalu'l-Dm Ruml, a Muslim mystic, who, in my opinion, was the smartest person who ever lived, next to Jesus. He said, "Your depression is connected to your insolence and refusal to praise." And by insolence, he was referring to narcissism or that kind of perverted pride which underlies depression.

DEPRESSION AND FANTASY

In my work with depressed people, I have frequently encountered what I call the Prince or Princess. The first time I had this experience, my patient was a woman. She had made good progress in dealing with her depression, thanks to her work with another psychiatrist, and came to me because she felt she had a little further to go. After we had been working for nearly a year, she was talking one day about a very complex problem with her children. The stakes seemed high and it was most unclear what she should do about it. In the midst of evaluating the problem, she exclaimed, "God, I'll be glad when therapy is over!" I said, "Why did you just say that?" And she said, "I'll be glad when therapy is over and I no longer have to agonize over these problems!''

I smelled a fantasy—that psychotherapy would take away not only all present but future pain—and this is a fantasy that is common in the Prince or Princess.

To explain how people can come to hold such a fantasy, I have to give a little background on child psychology. Infants during the first year of life, as best we can discern, come to learn what we call their ego boundaries. Before they learn this, they don't really recognize the difference between their hand and Mommy's hand, for example; they think that because they have a stomachache, Mommy has a stomachache, and the world has a stomachache. By the second year they learn their physical boundaries, although not yet the boundaries of their power, so they generally still go around thinking they are the center of the universe, with their parents and siblings and dogs and cats merely minions of their private royal army.

Then during the terrible twos, Mommy and Daddy start saying, ''No. No, Johnny, you can't do that. No. No, you can't do that, either. No, no, you can't do that, either. No. No. We love you very much, Johnny, and you're very important, but no, you can't do that. You're not the boss.'' Thus, in the course of a year, the child is psychologically demoted from a four-star general to a private. It is no wonder that it's a time of depression and tantrums, which is what the terrible twos are.

Nonetheless, if parents can be gentle with the child and support it as much as possible through this difficult period, by the time it leaves the terrible twos, it will have taken its first giant step out of narcissism. Unfortunately, this is not always the way it happens. Sometimes the parents are not gentle and do not support the child in this necessarily humiliating time, but instead aggravate the humiliation.

The woman who had the fantasy that she would no longer have to agonize about problems when psychotherapy was over had been raised in a home that was strict, to say the least. While she could not remember her terrible twos, she could remember the time when she was three or four and was subjected to a particular ritual whenever she did something wrong. She would be told to go and take down a switch that hung on the wall, carry it to her father, and present it to him. Then she would have to pull down her panties, hold up her skirt, bend over, and stand there while she was beaten until she had cried loudly and long enough that he stopped. Then she would have to pull up her panties and take the switch from her father and replace it on the wall. Then she would go to her mother to be consoled, and when she had been consoled sufficiently and had stopped crying, her mother would say, "Now get down on your knees and pray out loud to God for forgiveness." So she would get down on her knees and pray out loud for God's forgiveness, and when her prayers were judged by her mother to be sufficient in length, the mother would say, "Now you can get up and go over to your earthly father and ask him for his forgiveness." So she would go to her father, and if her petitions were sufficient, he would grant her his forgiveness, and the ritual would be over until the next time she did something wrong.

How do children survive that kind of treatment? The way they survive is not by giving up their infantile omnipotence and narcissism but by holding on to them. The mechanism for this is so specific that we psychiatrists have a name for it; it is called the "family romance.'' What such children do (and indeed, this is what my patient could remember doing) is to tell themselves, ''These people who say they are my parents really aren't my parents. In reality I am the daughter of the King and Queen, a child of royal blood, a Princess, and someday I will be recognized for who I am. Then I will come into my own.''

This is a very consoling fantasy to get children through such humiliation, except that as they grow significantly into adulthood—and by then the fantasy is much more subconscious—nobody has come to take them to the King and Queen, nobody has recognized them for who they feel they really are. So they become depressed. And what can lie at the base of the cognitive difficulty of depressives is this core fantasy that bad things shouldn't happen to them. Of course they selectively perceive the negative when they believe they should be exempted from it—and fail to perceive the positive which they feel should be their royal right.

There's a psychiatrist in Brazil named Norberto Keppe who suggests that the most common human mental illness is what he calls theomania: the delusion that we human beings can be God. Theomania is very much like the Prince or Princess fantasy although infinitely more ordinary. For example, a decade or so ago, I was working with a man who had a very deeply entrenched Christian identity. He had been a professional Christian youth worker in his twenties and was now a middle-aged businessman I'll call Joe Jones. At the time he came to see me, he was in league with a couple of unscrupulous people who were financing his business venture, and there was an enormous amount of pressure on him to sell out, to lie—specifically, to go to a hardware show with a product and pretend he had a patent, which he did not, in order to sell it. Had I been in his position, I would have been anxious myself, but this man was in unrelenting panic. Trying to console him one day, I said, "Joe, all that you can do is the best that you can do." And that is when he snapped, "The best that I can do isn't good enough for Joe Jones!"

It seemed a strange statement to make, so I asked, "What do you mean?" And he said, "It's not only necessary that I do the best job I can do, but it's also necessary that this business not fail. "

I said, "Listen, Joe, for all you know, the best thing that could happen to you in the long run would be for this business to fail. And for all we know, God wants this business to fail. Look, we are all of us actors in a wonderfully complex celestial drama, and the best we can hope for is to get little glimpses of what the drama is all about and how we might best play our roles. What I hear you saying, Joe, is that not only do you want to be the best actor you can be in this drama, but you also want to be the scriptwriter."

Joe is Everyman. We all go around suffering from theomania, the illusion that we can be the scriptwriter in the drama of our lives, and we become furious, depressed, or terrified when things don't go as we would have written the script or wanted them to go. In fact, many of us are never able to adjust to the reality that life is larger than something that is just our show. In this failure to adjust, we fail to learn. But for real learning and growing, we have to come to terms with the fact that, as someone once put it, "life is what happens when you've planned something else." Thank God!

CHAPTER ELEVEN

New Age: Symboline or Diaboline?

In the escalating search for road signs on the journey through the desert, many people have found themselves needing "religion," but unable to stomach what much of "organized religion" passes off as religion. This has led to the popularity of various cults and to an interest in Eastern philosophies evidenced by the popularity of such books as *The Tao of Pooh* and *The Te of Piglet, The Tibetan Book of the Dead,* and even *Am I a Hindu?*

Although the interest in Eastern philosophy has been around for a long time, it has recently been popularized by what has come to be known as the New Age movement. A great many people today are confused by the movement and I am frequently asked whether I consider it a force for the good or not. To answer that question, let me pose another: Is the New Age movement a force for integration or for separation?

I have two hobbies. One is collecting Freudian slips, and the other collecting light bulb jokes. And my two favorite light bulb jokes are, of course, religious light bulb jokes. The first is: "How many Episcopalians does it take to change a light bulb? Two. One to mix the martinis and one to call the electrician." The second is: "How many Zen Buddhists does it take to change a light bulb? Two. One to change the light bulb and one not to change the light bulb."

While that might strike you as funny, it is, in fact, a statement of integration and a very succinct way of defining paradox, of which Zen Buddhism has been my best teacher. I highly recommend Zen Buddhism for this very reason, since accepting the many paradoxes of life is essential to mental health.

I cannot stress enough how important thinking paradoxically is to me. I am very much like the professor of philosophy who was asked by one of his students, "Professor, it is said that you believe that the core of all truth is paradox. Is that correct?" And the professor answered, "Yes and no." Thus, to answer the question of whether the New Age movement is a force for integration or for separation, I am also going to answer yes and no.

THE AQUARIAN CONSPIRACY

A lot of people have questioned whether the New Age movement really exists at all. Perhaps it is somewhat mistitled, since the kinds of things that people who are in the New Age movement believe or are interested in have been around forever. But I think that there is a genuine New Age movement in that for the past thirty years, more and more people, a very significant portion of the population, have been turning to these beliefs and interests.

But when we call it a movement, I do not mean that it is an organized kind of movement. There have been many Christian fundamentalists who have declared it a satanic conspiracy to undermine Christian doctrine. It is because of this kind of thinking that Marilyn Ferguson, who authored a classic work on the New Age movement, called her book *The Aquarian Conspiracy*—very tongue in cheek, of course. She made the point very validly that it is not a conspiracy at all. People didn't get together and cook up this kind of thing. Like most important intellectual movements, the New Age movement sprang up spontaneously in response to the needs, pressures, and forces of the day. And thus it might be looked upon more as a revolutionary movement than an evolutionary one.

Like most revolutionary movements, New Age is primarily an upper-middle-class movement; it is not terribly important among the poor or blue-collar workers. And it is an international movement, not only an American or North American phenomenon. It is just as alive in places like Germany and England as it is in the United States.

Finally, and most important, the New Age movement is, in my opinion, a reaction against the institutional sins of Western civilization. Sins tend to be interrelated, and so, even though I may discuss them singly, keep in mind that they exist in conjunction with one another.

Please also keep in mind that not all institutional sins are ''Western.'' Institutional sexism is even more entrenched in the East than in the West. But, among other things, the New Age movement is a reaction against the sexism found in industry, in the church, in government, and as such it is a movement toward feminism.

A more "Western" sin is the emptiness of spirit and the arrogance, narcissism, and blasphemy of the Christian church. The New Age movement, consequently, is a movement away from Western religions to Eastern religions, to Buddhism, to Zen, to Taoism, to Hinduism, to Native American religions, or to the more feminist religions of the Mother Goddess and Wicca. And because organized religion has been very intolerant of beliefs other than its own, the New Age movement has tended to incorporate an extraordinary hodgepodge of ideas, including many esoteric notions ranging from astrology to astral projection to ethereal bodies. The list is almost endless.

The New Age movement is also a reaction against the sins of science, or at least science as it has been translated into technology, and those sins too are very real. Modern science has led us into a kind of excessive specialization which, in turn, tends to lead to a technological inhumanity. Anyone who has been hospitalized, getting the best of modern medical technology, is likely to have experienced some of this inhumanity in the name of "care" or "treatment." So, in reacting against technology, the New Age movement has tended away from Western medicine to, once again, Eastern medicine, to such things as acupuncture and chakras, to healing rituals of the Native Americans, to shamanism. Moving away from the specialization of Western medicine and technology, it has also paved the way for some very good holistic medicine and health through exercise. It has reintroduced herbal medicine and the idea of caring for the sick at home, and the hospice movement may be considered one of its very beneficial spin-offs.

And lastly, the New Age movement is a reaction

against the sins of capitalism, against the sins of imperialism and exploitation of the environment and of people. Again terribly real sins. So it is a movement away from exploitation and toward pacifism, toward the tolerance of diversity, and toward an ecological consciousness and balance with nature.

If anything characterizes the New Age movement, it is its openness to new ideas and new ways of doing things. And all that is wonderful. The problem—and it is the only problem, as far as I'm concerned, but it is huge—is what psychiatrists call reaction formation. Unfortunately, when you react against something that is sinful, you will often go to the other extreme, and you can get into as much trouble as you were in before. You can jump from the frying pan into the fire, or, as I often put it, throw out the baby with the bathwater.

Let me give you an example from my own history of what reaction formation can mean. My father was a judge and was in the habit of going on judicial tirades from time to time. Quite frequently, he would inappropriately bawl out desk clerks or hapless waiters. I can remember standing around at age twelve in restaurants or hotels, squirming with embarrassment as my father went on for fifteen or twenty minutes because some poor fellow had committed the most minor error. And I can remember vowing to myself that when I grew up, I was never going to make an ass out of myself like my father.

So when I did grow up, I never got angry in public. But as the years went on, I developed high blood pressure and my acquaintances started telling me that I was cold and distant and aloof and unfeeling. Finally, after I got into therapy, I realized that I had thrown the baby out with the bathwater—that in reacting against my father's inappropriate rages in public, I had cleansed myself, expurgated myself of all public anger. In fact, what I needed to get rid of was not all anger in public but simply *inappropriate* anger in public. Sometimes it is appropriate and necessary to get angry in public. But I had gone too far to the other extreme, and it took me some effort to relearn how to be angry, appropriately, in public. And it was only then that people started seeing me as less aloof and my blood pressure started to come down.

Unfortunately, the New Age movement has also gone to extremes. For instance, in reacting against male sexism, it has created a brand of radical feminism that can be not only distinctly unpleasant and unsettling but also rude and uncivil and even silly at times. I have spoken to audiences that comprised primarily radical feminists and it was difficult going indeed, even though I always go to some pains to use nonsexist language and to combat sexism.

Another example: In reacting against Judeo-Christian tradition the New Age movement has created a considerable amount of what I call spiritual confusion. In every large city in the United States you will find one or more organizations that I have come to call spiritual supermarkets. They put on various kinds of programs about virtually everything from Sufi dancing to the I Ching to Dionysian celebrations. You'll see everything there except Judaism or Christianity. And some people have been confused by this mixture, while others have used it as an excuse to run away from responsibility.

A few years after *The Road Less Traveled* was published, a man who was a kind of aging hippie came to see me. He was in his early forties, had a beard, long hair, a knapsack on his back, and he had hitchhiked to my home in Connecticut. He said he needed spiritual direction. He was at loose ends in his life and didn't know quite what he wanted to do. There was this Zen monastery in Vermont he was thinking of going to. On the other hand, there was a New Age commune out in Oregon that appealed to him. But then again there was this voice that said, "You ought to pay some attention to Christianity," which he hadn't done since he had run away from the Catholic church of his parents as soon as he could, at the age of sixteen. Anyway, what did I think he ought to do?

"Well," I said, "you'll have to tell me more about yourself before I can offer an opinion." So he proceeded to tell me that he had been married twice. He had two children by his first marriage and one by his second marriage, and he hadn't seen the children of the first marriage for over a dozen years, and hadn't seen the child from the second marriage for six years. When I asked why, he said, "It was a lot of hassle at the time of the divorces, and I figured it would really be better for the kids if I dropped out of the picture. But anyway, what shall I do about this spiritual groping?"

In answer, I told him that I had become a Christian since I wrote *The Road Less Traveled* and that I had done so in part because I had gradually come to believe in the meaningfulness of Christian doctrine. I explained that at the core of that doctrine there is the strange concept of sacrifice. I didn't think it meant that we need to sacrifice ourselves masochistically at every turn. But while I really didn't know yet what it means to be a Christian, I said, "At the very least what it means is that whenever there is a decision to be made, an alternative shouldn't be discarded simply because it *is* sacrificial."

213

When I said that, the man literally started to twitch and I thought he was going to have an epileptic seizure. I asked him what was the matter, and he said, "What you're doing is serious spiritual surgery on me." And I had to say, "I'm sorry it hurts."

He claimed that it was good for him. He wanted to come and see me again and he made an appointment. But then he called up two days later to cancel it. I suspect that rather than attempting to reestablish a relationship with his children, he opted for the New Age commune in Oregon.

THE WRONG SIN

It is my own particular belief that Christian doctrine, on the whole, approaches reality more closely than do the other great religions, although I also believe that on occasion the others may come a bit closer. In any case, there is a great deal of good in Christian thought that should not be dismissed. In my opinion, the New Age movement has been reacting against the wrong sin. The sin of Christianity has not been the sin of doctrine. It has been the sin of practice—a failure to integrate its behavior with its theology. As G. K. Chesterton put it, the greatest problem with Christianity is not that it has been tried and found wanting, but that it has hardly been tried at all.

The New Age movement, however, has reacted not only against the way Christians have behaved but against Christian theology as well, which the sinful Christian behavior does not embody. And in so doing New Agers have often thrown the baby out with the bathwater. Of course, not all of them dismiss Christianity. Some embrace it, but in the process of marrying it with Eastern religions, they not infrequently end up with something that is an unfortunate hybrid.

In moving away from Judeo-Christian theology to Eastern religions, New Agers also seem to have a tendency to advertise those religions as leading to the greater spiritual advancement. Stage Two people in every religion claim that their beliefs are the only true beliefs, and the reality is that at our own community-building workshops, we suffer at least as much from New Age fundamentalists as we do from Old Age ones. While as a whole it is characterized by openness to new ideas, there are many people in the New Age movement who are fundamentalists or inerrantists and are no more advanced than Christians of the same ilk. Some are what I call "herbal fundamentalists." They insist not only that there be herbal tea present, but that everybody at the workshop ought to drink it.

This I would not call tolerance. On the other hand, there are people in the movement who get into what I call tolerance in the extreme, which can result in a kind of inappropriate individualism. In one community-building workshop, we were screening a possible future workshop leader who said, "In community anything is appropriate." We had to teach him that in community not everything is appropriate. People cannot be in community who think it is appropriate to hit others or to verbally abuse them or champion a hidden agenda.

This excessive tolerance can also be seen in the real inability of many "liberals" to work together. Before Lily and I started the Foundation for Community Encouragement, we first considered a foundation that would work to unify the five hundred different peace organizations in this country. But gradually, as I played that scenario out in my mind, it became clear that any foundation we might start for that purpose would simply become the five hundred and first peace organization. Because even the peace organizations haven't yet learned how to work together, the task we eventually decided to invest our time and money in—community building—had to come first.

THE ISSUE OF EVIL

One area where Christian theology and the New Age movement tend to part company radically concerns the issue of evil. Christian doctrine holds that evil is real. Eastern religions do not consider it to be real. They consider it to be illusion or false knowledge, what they call maya.

I do not claim there is nothing to this view. There is no doubt in my mind that by thinking of evil we can create it. If we read the demonic into everything with which we disagree—as many Stage Two religious folk are prone to do—then we will cause fragmentation and hostility rather than healing. Through the New Age movement, however, the simplistic idea has spread that if we could just change our thinking, we would realize there's no such thing as evil in the world. It would all just go away, vanish. But the reality is that there really are people out there who like to maim, to torture, and to crush other people. There are people who want war because they profit from war. And you can get into serious trouble if you believe that there aren't. Because sooner or later you will be accosted with real evil, and dealing with it will not be as easy as some New Age books imply.

The one New Age book that has attracted the most

attention, and the one I am most often asked about, is *A Course in Miracles*. It is a very good book, filled with a lot of first-rate psychiatric wisdom. But *A Course in Miracles* also denies the reality of evil, saying that evil is unreal, a kind of figment of our imagination. This is not all that far from the truth, because evil does have a great deal to do with unreality. In fact, in my book *People of the Lie,* I defined Satan as "a real spirit of unreality." So evil does have a great deal to do with unreality—that is, with lies and untruth. But that doesn't mean that it in itself doesn't exist.

While *A Course in Miracles* purports to be Christian, it distorts Christian doctrine. It is not all the truth; rather, it is a half-truth, and in failing to deal with the problem of evil, it leaves out a major part of the picture. It runs with only one side of the "paradox" of evil.

The denial of evil is such a characteristic pitfall of the New Age movement that it has given rise to the one New Age joke I know. It was quite properly told to me by a New Age woman herself, who recounted how three clergy were sitting down in Hell: a Catholic priest, a Jewish rabbi, and a New Age minister. They begin to talk about what they are doing down there and the Catholic priest confesses, "Back on earth I used to be called a whiskey priest. I just loved my booze too much, and that's why I'm here in Hell. How about you, Rabbi, what are you in here for?" And the rabbi says, "I have to confess that I had this thing about ham sandwiches. I just couldn't leave them alone." And then the two of them turn to the New Age minister and ask him, "What about you? What are you doing down here in Hell?" And he answers, "This isn't Hell and I'm not the least bit warm."

THE SINS OF TECHNOLOGY

A similar problem has occurred in the New Age reaction against technology. It has tended to throw out scientific rigor. The scientific method, as I have explained, is only a collection of procedures and conventions that we have developed over the centuries in order to combat our very human tendency to want to deceive ourselves, and we have developed such procedures in the interest of something higher than our immediate intellectual or emotional comfort. Thus, the scientific method is a principled, highly disciplined kind of behavior, and represents a very holy pursuit after truth.

But in reacting against the sins of Western civilization, New Age has tended to throw out the scientific method. It is another example of throwing out the baby with the bathwater. The sin of technology is not the scientific method but the way that science has been translated by industry and government into technology.

The New Age movement in its reaction formation tends to exhibit a certain lack of "scientific" discernment, in matters of both theology and science. A friend of mine refers to California, the heart of the New Age movement, as Mars' Hill. It is a reference to what Saint Paul said in Athens when he went to Greece to preach. Paul was often an abrasive man, but he could also be a bit of a smoothie. And so when he reached the top of Mars' Hill, he began by saying he could see that the Athenians were a very spiritual people because, climbing up the hill, he had seen statues of a thousand different gods. And only a very spiritual people could have a thousand different gods.

This same lack of discernment among New Agers can lead to a lot of pretty flaky stuff. Some in California would be well advised to imitate those from Missouri, the "Show Me" state. The expression "I'm from Missouri" refers to an often healthy and discerning skepticism. I believe that before you undertake any adventure, and certainly any spiritual journey, you've got to know something about how to discern what is healthy and what is dangerous.

Golf is a great metaphor for this lesson. Playing a game of golf is an adventure, and in that sense it is fun. It can be more fun if you take risks and try new things, but there comes a point when the more chances you take, the worse golf you are going to play. Sometimes it is necessary to play it safe.

For example, the pin is often placed on the part of the green that is likely to cause golfers the most trouble; there is a steep cliff on one side, a sand trap in front, and maybe another steep cliff right in the back. A pro would probably go straight for the pin, but the pro is one in ten thousand golfers. And out of ten thousand golfers, probably nine thousand would be downright stupid to go for the pin. I think the rule for playing good golf is not to go for the pin, but to analyze the hole and work within your limitations. That is the rule, except on those rare occasions when you have a feeling you can beat the rule. Your intuition says go for it, and that is exactly what you should do. Take the risk.

This applies to one's spiritual life as well. But the New Age movement tends to encourage always going for the pin, adventuring without discernment, which has gotten people into trouble. That is why some have quipped that Shirley MacLaine should more aptly have titled her distinctly New Age autobiography not *Out on a Limb* but *Out on a Broken Limb*.

HERESY

Until about fifteen years ago, I believed heresy was a totally arcane subject that properly belonged back in the Middle Ages, along with the Inquisition, and had no relevance to our modern world. But then I began working in the hospital with a seriously disturbed "New Age" woman who had been involved with a whole variety of cults. By virtue of the intensity of her spiritual confusion, there was a priest who was serving me as a consultant on the case. Because the matter of religion was involved, I asked her one day, "Tell me about Jesus.

She proceeded to draw a cross on a piece of paper with circles in all quadrants, saying, "There are three Jesuses up here on the top part of the cross, and three down here on the bottom, and three on this arm, and three on that arm."

Sometimes it is necessary to be a bit confrontational. "Cut out that stuff," I ordered, and then asked, "How did He die?"

"He was crucified," she answered.

Something—perhaps the fact that she did everything she could to avoid pain—propelled me to inquire, "Did it hurt?"

"Oh no," she responded.

"What do you mean, it didn't hurt?" I persisted. "How could it not have hurt?"

"Oh," she replied happily, "He was just so highly developed in His Christ consciousness that He was able to project Himself into His astral body and take off from there.''

This seemed to me a wacky sort of answer, but I couldn't make any more of it than that until that night when, because it was so strange, I recounted it to my priest consultant, and he immediately said, ''Oh, that's Docetism.''

''What on earth is Docetism?'' I inquired.

''It was one of the very early church heresies,'' he explained to me. ''The Docetists were a group of early Christians who believed that Jesus was totally divine and His humanity was simply an appearance.''

It is important to understand here that Christian heresy is something that only Christians can be guilty of. There are other kinds of heresies we shall address shortly. But Christian heresy is something that is put forth in the name of Christian doctrine but that seriously undermines what the doctrine is all about. It is not difficult to see, then, why Docetism is a heresy. If Jesus was totally divine and His humanity simply an appearance, then His suffering on the cross—as my patient believed—was nothing more than a divine charade, and this whole business of sacrifice that lies at the center of Christian doctrine is nothing but a celestial sham by which so many have been taken in.

Heresy most commonly arises when we run with just one side of a paradox. It is also Christian heresy to believe the opposite of Docetism: namely, that Jesus was totally human, and that His divinity was nothing more than appearance. For if we believe that Jesus was simply another rather wise, ''self-actualized,'' but otherwise perfectly ordinary mortal man, then we

221

must conclude that God did not "come down to live and die as one of us."

So what we are left with at the center of Christian doctrine—whether one cares to believe it or not—is a paradox: that Jesus was paradoxically both human and divine—not fifty percent one and fifty percent the other but, as the doctrine states, "fully human and fully divine."

Since that time I have come to realize that most of the old Christian heresies are alive and well in all manner of places. There are, for instance, two schools of theology called Immanence and Transcendence. Immanence focuses upon the indwelling divinity within human beings, the God of the Holy Spirit or what Quakers call "the inner light." Transcendence, on the other hand, focuses upon the divinity external to us humans: our Father who art in Heaven, or the big cop up in the sky. Both of these foci are necessary. Whenever people run solely with one or the other, they can get into trouble.

If we believe that God resides totally inside of us, then every thought or feeling that we have can assume the status of revelation. This has been a problem with some of the New Age denominations that are referred to as "New Thought" churches. If we believe the opposite, however, and think that God resides totally up there and out there, then we have the problem of how on earth God ever communicates with us mere mortals except through weird prophets like Moses and Jesus, whose words and deeds are then interpreted to us by a priestly class. This can lead to what I sometimes call "the heresy of orthodoxy" and such things as the Inquisition, where the Inquisitors were, of course, far worse heretics than

222

anyone they were torturing or burning in the name of heresy—if for no other reason than the fact that they were killing the indwelling divinity of their victims. Indeed, an exclusive focus on transcendence is a heresy that some ultratraditional, right-wing Catholics or fundamentalists still fall into.

So what we are left with, once again, is another paradox: that God resides both inside of us in His or Her still, small voice and, simultaneously, outside of us in all of His or Her transcendent, magnificent otherness.

Let me give a final example of two different styles of thinking that are also quite prevalent in these modern days. About fifteen hundred years ago there was a workaholic Irish monk by the name of Pelagius, who taught his followers that salvation was achieved by doing lots of good works. That has since come to be known as the heresy of Pelagianism because it can get us into various kinds of difficulty. It can lead us not only to become workaholics ourselves but also to conclude that salvation is purely something that we earn, and that the grace of God has nothing to do with it. This can further encourage us to a certain kind of unwarranted pride in our ''own'' achievements.

Around three hundred years ago in Europe there was a group of Christians who believed the opposite: namely, that salvation was the result of grace alone. They became known as the Quietists, because they sat around quietly waiting for grace to happen. Because this is not the kind of doctrine that would encourage the sorts of social activism Jesus urged us toward, Quietism is also considered a heresy. So, once again, we are pushed to conclude that salvation is the result of some paradoxical mixture of both grace and good works for which we do not have—nor will we ever—any mathematical formula.

NON-CHRISTIAN HERESIES

Other religions can have heresies and may even share them with Christianity. For instance, the struggle over the paradox of grace and good works has been just as much a problem for Muslims as it has for Christians. In fact, the best advice I know on the subject came from Muhammad, who said, "Trust in God, but tie your camel first."

There is also such a thing as secular heresy. The ethic of rugged individualism is the best example. This ethic holds that we are called to become individuals. And that is partly true. Carl Jung said the whole goal of psychospiritual growth was individuation, the ability to be separate from our own parents and to think for ourselves. We are called to become independent and stand on our own two feet, to become captains of our ship, if not necessarily masters of our own destiny. We are called to those things. But rugged individualism rejects the whole other side of the coin, which Jung also talked about. We're called to come to terms with our limitations, our brokenness, our inevitable mutual interdependence. As do other kinds of heresies, rugged individualism neglects that whole other side of the paradox.

This leads to terrible pain—people sitting next to each other in the same pew, hiding behind their masks of composure, pretending they've got it all together, because we're told we ought to have it all together. But in fact, nobody's got it all together, and as a result of the ethic of rugged individualism huge numbers feel that they're not able to talk to each other about the things that are most important to them. It is so isolating, being in our little airtight compartments.

To escape heresy, we must accept paradox. Thinking with integrity is paradoxical thinking. And it is not only necessary that we think with integrity, it's also necessary that we act with integrity. Behaving with integrity is "praxis," a term that was popularized initially by Marxists, and since then has been picked up by liberation theologists. Praxis refers to the integration of your practice with your belief system. As Gandhi said: "What is faith worth if it is not translated into action?" Obviously, we have to integrate our behavior with our theology in order to become people of integrity. Too often that is not done, whatever the religious belief.

HERESY IS ALIVE AND WELL IN MODERN CHRISTIANITY

I do not wish to lay the blame for heresy on New Age churches, because in fact heresies prevail in formal, traditional Christian churches. One more evident than any other I call pseudo-Docetism. Christians guilty of this heresy have had enough religious training to know the paradoxical reality of Jesus being both human and divine, but put ninety-nine percent of their money on His divinity, and only one percent on His humanity. This leads to the excuse that we can't really be expected to behave like Jesus because it places us way down here, ninety-nine percent human, and Him way up there, beyond identification or imitation.

Here is an example of how bad this has become. Not

long ago I participated in a conference of Christian therapists and counselors, where the speaker, Harvey Cox, a Baptist theologian, told the Gospel story of Jesus being called to resuscitate the daughter of a wealthy Roman. As Jesus is going to the Roman's house, a woman who has been hemorrhaging for years reaches out from the crowd and touches His robe. He feels her touch and turns around and asks, "Who touched me?" The woman comes forward and begs Him to cure her and He does, and then goes on to the house of the Roman whose daughter had died.

After telling the story, Cox asked this audience of six hundred mostly Christian professionals whom they identified with. When he asked who identified with the bleeding woman, about a hundred raised their hands. When he asked who identified with the anxious Roman father, more of the rest raised their hands. When he asked who identified with the curious crowd, most raised their hands. But when he asked who identified with Jesus, only six people raised their hands.

Something is very wrong here. Of six hundred more or less professional Christians, only one out of a hundred identified with Jesus. Maybe more actually did but were afraid to raise their hands lest that seem arrogant. But again something is wrong with our concept of Christianity if it seems arrogant to identify with Jesus. That is exactly what we are supposed to do! We're supposed to identify with Jesus, act like Jesus, be like Jesus. That is what Christianity is supposed to be about—the imitation of Christ.

Another brand of heresy has to do with the Christian interpretation of blasphemy, which is the violation of the Second Commandment, "Thou shalt not take the name of the Lord thy God in vain.'' Most Christians I meet as I go around the country erroneously interpret this to mean that you shouldn't swear or use dirty language. But that is not what blasphemy is about. Blasphemy is just the opposite. It is using sweet religious language to cloak irreligious behavior.

I once attended a conference where the great Sufi, Idries Shah, was lecturing. And after he had lectured twice over the course of two days, he finally said, ''You know that I have been talking to you for four hours now, and I have not yet once used the words 'God' or 'love.' We Sufis do not use these words lightly. They are *sacred*.''

Unfortunately, these words are not sacred to many Christians. I spent a weekend with a born-again couple in South Carolina whose every other sentence was God did this and God did that, and God would do this and God would do that, interspersed with nasty gossip about who was sleeping with whom and who wasn't going to church and whose children had gone sour. When I finally got out of there after three days, I thought if I'd heard God did this and God did that one more time, I would have puked! Their sin was even graver to me than petty gossip because I felt all their ''God talk'' was blasphemous—the use of ''the name of the Lord'' in such a way as to trivialize God.

I do not think that the order of the Ten Commandments is accidental. Violation of the First—idolatry—tends to be at the root of all sin. But violation of the Second—blasphemy—is the sin of sins, the lie of lies. It is the pretense of piety accompanied by a total lack of praxis: the ultimate lack of integrity, the refusal even to attempt to integrate one's behavior with one's theology.

227

COMMUNITY VERSUS CULT

So there are many traps for traditional Christians as well as for New Agers. One open to both is the phenomenon of cults. I do not, in any way, object to people wanting to live together in community. That is a holy calling as far as I am concerned. But there is a big difference between a community and a cult. Community draws people in by its interconnectedness; community applies no pressure for people to stay; community glories in the extraordinary differences of its members. Cults, on the other hand, are characterized by the brainwashing of their members, by a tremendous pressure to join and not leave, and by a certain sameness of the people in them.

To help make the distinction, I have identified ten characteristics of what makes a cult:

1. Idolatry of a single charismatic leader

The Reverend Sun Myung Moon, acclaimed by Moonies as "The Lord of the Second Advent," is an obvious, overtly religious example of such idolatry. So were Jim Jones and David Koresh, charismatic men who led their followers to disaster and death. There are many "gurus" who encourage adoration of themselves.

2. A revered inner circle

Not even the most ambitious charismatic leader can single-handedly manage an organization beyond a certain size. He or she needs trusted disciples. Generally, all large cults have an inner circle of members who are revered by others almost as much as is the leader. They are held in awe; they are feared; they are envied; they are gossiped about. This revered inner circle is not an utterly distinctive feature of cults; it exists to a greater or lesser degree in any large organization, government, business corporation, university, or church. The question is the degree of reverence or awe and hence the potential for the abuse of power.

3. Secrecy of management

One of the distinguishing features of cults is the great secrecy with which these inner circles operate. Again, this secrecy is characteristic of a great many nonreligious organizations. Think of the executive branch of our government and its obsession with secret documents and security classifications. Think of the industrial secrets of our business corporations. Think of the boardrooms, the smoke-filled rooms, the seemingly casual breakfast meetings that really count. But cult leaders do not maintain even the pretense of accountability for their actions.

4. Financial evasiveness

Some years ago, Lily and I had the opportunity to spend the better part of a day with the top leadership of a New Age peace organization. One of the many disheartening things about that day, which led us to conclude that the organization was a cult, was the group's evasiveness concerning its finances. Why the secrecy? we wondered. The organization was nonprofit, and presumably its finances were a matter of public record and could be investigated by anyone who wanted to take the trouble. I could only assume that the secrecy characteristic of cult leadership was so habitual that it unnecessarily contaminated this most important, public area. It was not the only way in which this organization seemed evasive to us; it was just the most surprising. In any case, financial evasiveness, for whatever reason, does seem to be a characteristic of many cults.

5. Dependency

Perhaps the major reason cults are justifiably feared is that their authoritarian leadership nurtures the dependency of the followers. Rather than encouraging their followers to become a group of all leaders, cults tend to discourage the capacity of their members to think for themselves. This used to be a problem in the Catholic church. Now it can be a problem of flocking to the East for our spiritual answers. It is actually a tradition of Hinduism for its gurus to teach their disciples to look upon them as gods.

6. Conformity

This, to me, is the saddest feature of cults. The leaders of the peace organization I mentioned earlier struck me with their sameness. They varied in age from thirty to seventy; they were men and women; some were dressed formally, others informally. Yet I have never sat in a meeting in the military or government or anywhere else with twenty people who seemed so oppressively the same.

7. Special language

It is natural for any group of people who work closely and intensively with each other to develop a special internal language—that is, a set of words that have a special meaning to them often incomprehensible to people outside the organization. The more closely the organization moves toward being a cult, the more special this internal language tends to become. Ultimately, it is like a secret language, known only to initiates, and quite untranslatable. For instance, I receive mail from a variety of New Age organizations attempting to enlist my interest. They might succeed if I could take them seriously, but I have a hard time connecting with phrases like "resonating core groups" or "reevolutionizing." Such groups have become so imbued with their special language that they have lost the capacity to communicate effectively with the outside world.

8. Dogmatic doctrine

One cult used to be fond of saying that they were in the process of "developing" their theology and that they wanted to enlist the aid of outsiders, such as myself, in this development. I think it was largely a ploy. As far as I could assess the situation, their theology was already quite developed and most of its doctrines had long since become doctrinaire.

9. Heresy

All organizations exist in relationship to God, consciously or unconsciously, whether they like it or not. In the case of a business corporation, it is usually a relationship of at least passive denial of God. In the case of a satanic cult, it is a relationship of active, vehement denial. The relationship between cults and God is virtually always out of kilter and heretical.

10. God in captivity

In their skewed relationship to God and their satisfaction with dogmatism, cults—one way or another— feel they have God all sewn up. They have captured God. But the reality is that God is not ours to possess, we are His/Hers to be possessed by, individually and collectively.

If you are trying to evaluate a particular organization, let me point out that to be a cult, a group does not have to satisfy all ten criteria. If it meets three or four, I would be suspicious. It is also important to realize that cults are a dime a dozen and that a great many businesses are cults. I believe that IBM used to be something of a cult, exerting tremendous pressure on its employees to dress the same, look the same, and behave the same.

It has been pointed out to me that the Catholic church fits most of the above criteria. However, I do not believe that the American Catholic church is a cult. It may have been a cult before the Vatican II Council in the 1960s, but Vatican II totally revolutionized Catholicism in this country. In a cult the authority system is totally accepted and never challenged. The authority system in the American Catholic church is now being challenged every day of the week and twice on Sunday. The women's movement in the Catholic church is one of the most active in any Christian church today. There is a great deal of turmoil, but also a great deal of variety in how individual churches practice their faith, ranging from very conservative to very liberal. And this is why I joke that the current, very conservative pope is doing his best to annul Vatican II.

The credit for the incredible transformation of the Catholic church in recent years goes, of course, to Pope John XXIII, who was originally elected as only an interim pope. At the time of his election, the College of Cardinals had a hell of a time agreeing on a suitable candidate, and finally, as a compromise, they decided to elect one of the oldest and most inoffensive of men. John, in his seventies, was overweight and seemed like a sweet old man who wouldn't last long or do much. Within a year of being elected, however, he had initiated Vatican II, and when asked why such a council was necessary, he threw open one of the ancient windows in the Vatican and exclaimed, ''Fresh air! Fresh air!''

NEW AGE AS A SYMBOLINE FORCE

Fresh air is what the New Age movement at its best is about. And while I have so far focused on the "diaboline" aspects of the New Age movement, I firmly believe that the sins New Age is reacting against are very real sins, and that they should be reacted against. The virtues of the New Age movement are absolutely enormous, if the problem of reaction formation can be avoided. In its "symboline" aspects—and that is precisely the right word—New Age is a movement in the direction of integration and integrity, and you see the results. You see it in holistic medicine, which integrates different kinds and aspects of medicine rather than being excessively specialized. You see it in the ecology movement, which integrates the contributions of all living things to the cycle of life. You see it in a much more global kind of thinking than the old mind-set we were once used to.

For example, some years ago, before the Berlin Wall fell, I had the good fortune to meet in an intimate group for three days with two Soviet citizens, one of whom was a high-ranking member of the Central Committee of the Communist Party, who had come here to try and convince us in America that *glasnost* was a real phenomenon. At that point most Americans thought it was some kind of propaganda trick the Russians had cooked up. But through meeting with them in community, I became convinced that it was real.

Shortly after that, I was at a conference where Jack Anderson, the famous Washington columnist, was speaking. Anderson is a man who has done a lot of good things in his life, but he still had an old mind-set. During the question-and-answer period, he was asked about *glasnost* and he said, knowing the facts, that *glasnost* was a very real phenomenon. He commented quite accurately that there was a lot of opposition to it in the Soviet Union, particularly from an organization made up largely of older people who were profoundly anti-Semitic and who were fighting against *glasnost*. There was also a great deal of resistance to it, he commented, within the very strong and entrenched Soviet bureaucracy. And then Anderson said, "Thank God the Russians have an even worse bureaucracy than we do."

This is what I mean by the old mind-set—when we actually thank God that other people are worse off than we. I thank God that this old competitive mind-set has, indeed, begun to change. And in a paradigm shift—which is another popular term in the New Age movement—we do need a kind of glasnost in America, an openness of our own. We need to move away from competition and compartmentalization toward greater integration in all aspects of our social and spiritual lives.

REVOLUTION OR REFORM

Having answered the question "Is the New Age movement symboline or diaboline?" with a yes and no, I am still left pondering its future. Is it going to be a revolution or a reformation? If it swings to the side of revolution, I think it is going to fail and be dangerous. If, on the other hand, it can keep to a path of reformation, then I think it will become a very holy thing, because we are in great need of reform.

Reformation is more difficult than revolution. It's often easier just to do something different than to hang in there and bring about reform. And the sins of the Old Age that the New Age movement has tackled are not easy to reform. Take medicine, for example. I very much believe in holistic medicine, but it is not cheap medicine. In fact, good holistic medicine is much more expensive than our typically specialized assembly-line kind of medicine. There are also a lot of New Age fads associated with it, and a lot of charlatans making heaps of money pretending to be practitioners of holistic medicine.

I ponder sometimes whether FCE—the Foundation for Community Encouragement which Lily and I helped start in 1984—is a New Age organization. In some ways it is. One of our clearly stated values, for instance, is "Openness to new ideas." On the same list of values, however, is another that reads: "Valid data"— a value of very traditional science and business practice. We must wage an ongoing, paradoxical struggle to keep such values integrated.

Integrity is not easy. It is always painful. And it is much more difficult to behave with integrity than without it. Since integrity is never painless, reformation is much more difficult than revolution. Whether the New Age movement is going to be saving or damning will come down to whether it is a movement of revolution or of reformation—whether it can motivate the people attracted to its new ideas to do the painful work and practice the discipline required not to throw the baby out with the bathwater, to integrate the best of the new with the best of the old.

CHAPTER TWELVE

Sexuality and Spirituality

The notion that there is a relationship between sexuality and spirituality is shocking to some people—at least to those who have never read the Song of Solomon in the Bible, which begins "Let him kiss me with the kisses of his mouth . . ." This Song of Songs, as it is more properly titled, is an exquisite, erotic duet between God and His or Her people. There is, however, a particular brand of religion that identifies sex and sexuality with the devil, who supposedly tempts us with lust and the sinful pleasures of the flesh. In that context the only possible relationship there can be between sexuality and spirituality is one of war, in which one side must win out over the other. But my own view is that insofar as there is conflict between sexuality and spirituality, it is more in the nature of a lovers' quarrel or a sibling rivalry, both of which to some extent can be outgrown.

If we begin by asking what sexuality is, right away we run into a scientific stone wall. Here at the end of the twentieth century, we know how to blow ourselves off the face of the earth, but we can't even begin, from a scientific point of view, to understand what the nonanatomical differences or similarities are between men and women. I'm afraid that mythology once again has much more to tell us about the nature of sexuality than does our science.

One of the basic themes in mythology is fear on the part of the gods that human beings are becoming like them, and the myth of sexuality is a variant of this same theme. This myth tells us that, at the beginning, human beings were androgynous, unified creatures. But as such, they were rapidly gaining in power and were about to encroach upon the gods. So the gods split human beings into halves—male and female. And as half creatures, we were no longer capable of competing with the gods. Yet we were also left feeling incomplete, yearning for our lost wholeness, forever searching for our other half, hoping that in the moment of sexual union with our other half we might reexperience the lost bliss of our near godlike totality.

So, at least according to the myth, our sexuality arises out of a sense of incompleteness and is manifested by an urge toward wholeness and a yearning for the godhead. But what is our spirituality if not the same thing? What is our spirituality if not something that arises out of a sense of incompleteness and is manifested by an urge toward wholeness and a yearning for the godhead?

Sexuality and spirituality are not, of course, exactly the same thing. They are not identical twins, but they are kissing cousins, and they arise out of the same kind of ground, not only in myth but in actual human experience.

The fact is that sex is the closest that many people ever come to a spiritual experience. Indeed, it is because it is a spiritual experience of sorts that so many chase after it with a repetitive, desperate kind of abandon. Often, whether they know it or not, they are searching for God. It is no accident that even atheists and agnostics will, at the moment of orgasm, routinely cry out, "Oh God!"

ORGASM AS A MYSTICAL EXPERIENCE

The great psychologist Abraham Maslow one day decided, instead of studying sick people, to study particularly healthy people—the one in ten thousand who seemed to have gotten most of it together, who seemed to have fullfilled their potential, become most fully human. These he called "self-actualized people." (Personally, I would prefer the term "co-actualized.") Studying them, he discerned some thirteen things they had in common. And one of them was that they routinely experienced orgasm as a spiritual, even mystical event.

Again, that word "mystical" is more than an analogy. Throughout the ages mystics have spoken of an ego death as a necessary part of the spiritual, mystical journey, or even as the goal, the end of the mystical journey itself. And you may know that the French have traditionally referred to orgasm as *la petite mort,* or "the little death."

The subjective quality of the orgasmic experience is, of course, highly dependent on the quality of the relationship of the partners involved. So, if it is the best possible orgasm you are after, then the best way to achieve it is with someone who is deeply beloved to you. But while a relationship with a beloved other is necessary to bring us to the very highest mystical heights of the orgasmic experience, once we reach those heights we actually lose the awareness of our partner. At that brief peak point of little death, we forget who and where we are. And in a very real sense, I think, this is because we have left this earth and entered God's country.

As Ananda Coomaraswami put it, "At the moment of mutual climax, each as individuals has no more significance to the other than the gates of Heaven for the one within." Or as Joseph Campbell paraphrased it, "When one has lost oneself in the rapture of love, the partner is of no more importance than the portals of the temple through which one has passed to the altar."

So the sexual experience is potentially religious. Is the religious experience sexual? I don't believe it is an accident that throughout history most of the very best erotic poetry has been written by monks and nuns. You may already be familiar with the famous "Dark Night" poem of Saint John of the Cross:

1. One dark night,
    fired with love's urgent longings
    —ah, the sheer grace!—
    I went out unseen,
    my house being now all stilled.

2. In darkness and secure,
    by the secret ladder, disguised,
    —ah, the sheer grace!—
    in darkness and concealment,
    my house being now all stilled.

3. On that glad night,
    in secret, for no one saw me,
    nor did I look at anything,

with no other light or guide
than the one that burned in my heart.

4. This guided me
more surely than the light of noon
to where he was waiting for me,
—him I knew so well—
there in a place where no one appeared.

Note the mixing of the sexes in this next stanza:

5. O guiding night!
O night more lovely than the dawn!
O night that has united
the Lover with his beloved,
transforming the beloved in her Lover.

6. Upon my flowering breast
which I kept wholly for him alone,
there he lay sleeping,
and I caressing him
there in a breeze from the fanning cedars.

7. When the breeze blew from the turret,
as I parted his hair,
it wounded my neck
with its gentle hand,
suspending all my senses.

8. I abandoned and forgot myself,
laying my face on my Beloved;
all things ceased;
I went out from myself,
leaving my cares forgotten among the lilies.

I believe that the final stanza of this poem, which describes the mystical union possible between human beings and God, is also as fine a description of orgasm as anything in literature: "I abandoned and forgot myself . . . all things ceased . . . I went out from myself . . ."

I have learned in my encounters with monks and nuns that the best monk or nun is someone who loves God the most passionately. And in order to love God passionately, one has to be a passionate, sexual person. How is it then that just such people choose chastity or celibacy?

There are two reasons. The first, if you will pardon the pun, is that sex can screw up relationships. As soon as we make a sexual object of another person, there is a profound tendency to use him or her. Although we've got somewhat differing masculine and feminine styles of doing this, we each have a tendency to use the sex object in our lives in ways that are covertly, if not overtly, manipulative and self-serving.

There have been experiments with noncelibate convents and monasteries, but thus far they have all been failures. Therefore, those who firmly resolve to relate with their fellow human beings in an unfailingly healing fashion usually decide that a highly restrained sexuality, such as celibacy or chastity, is the price they must pay. And often they find the price well worth it

THE ILLUSION OF ROMANTIC LOVE

In *The Road Less Traveled*, I drew a sharp distinction between love (which I defined as concern for the spiritual growth of another) and romantic love (which I have come to understand as a form of narcissism). The whole American ideal of romantic love holds that it ought to be somehow possible for Cinderella to ride off with her prince into the sunset of endless orgasms. It is an illusion. Romantic love is preferable to what preceded it in history—namely, a culture of marriage by arrangement. But nonetheless, anyone who believes that permanent romance in a relationship is a perpetual possibility is doomed to perpetual disappointment. In fact, it is the search for God in human romantic relationships that is, I think, one of the greatest problems we have in this and other cultures.

What we do is to look to our spouse or lover to be a god unto us. We look to our spouse or lover to meet all of our needs, to fulfill us, to bring us a lasting Heaven on earth. And it never works. And among the reasons it never works—whether or not we're aware when we do this—is that we are violating the First Commandment, which says, "I am the Lord thy God, and thou shalt not have any other gods before me."

It is, however, also very natural that we should do this. It is very natural to want to have a tangible God, one whom we can not only see and touch but also hold and embrace and sleep with and perhaps even possess. So, we keep looking to our spouse or lover to be a god unto us, and in the process, we forget about the true God.

Thus the other reason the profoundly religious so often choose celibacy is that they do not want to be distracted from their love of God. They do not want to fall prey to the idolatry of human romantic love. They know that, as Saint Augustine said, "You made us for Yourself, dear Lord, and we cannot find true rest except in You." And that it is possible, if their number-one relationship is with God, that they may not need to seek another.

THE SEXINESS OF SPIRITUALITY

It is not my intent to make an impassioned plea for celibacy as a necessity for spiritual growth. On the contrary, I celebrate not only sexuality but sex. I like sex and I like other people to have sex.

About a dozen years ago, after many months of working with a rigid, frigid woman in her mid-thirties, I had the opportunity to witness her undergo a sudden and quite profound Christian conversion. And within three weeks of that conversion, she became orgasmic for the first time in her life. Could the timing have been accidental? I doubt it. As a friend of mine once put it, ''The sexual and the spiritual parts of our personality lie so close together that it is hardly possible to arouse one without arousing the other.'' I do not think it an accident that when this woman became able to give herself wholeheartedly to God, in very short order she became able to give herself wholeheartedly to a human partner, praise the Lord!

I have another friend, a priest, who actually uses this phenomenon as a yardstick of conversion. He tells me that if a conversion occurs in a previously sexually repressed individual and is not accompanied by some kind of sexual awakening or blossoming, then he has reason to doubt the depth of the conversion.

So it is that you hear stories about ministers who become involved with female parishioners. Ministers and other people in similar positions tend to be sitting ducks when such passions are aroused. And I will confess that when I was practicing psychotherapy, any time I got on the same spiritual wavelength with a female patient of mine under the age of ninety, I had to watch my step.

THE UNIVERSAL PROBLEM

Sex is a problem for everyone. Sex is a problem for children, sex is a problem for adolescents, sex is a problem for young adults, sex is a problem for middle-aged adults, sex is a problem for elderly adults. Sex is a problem for celibates, sex is a problem for married people, sex is a problem for single people, sex is a problem for straight people, sex is a problem for gay people. Sex is a problem for bricklayers and plumbers, sex is a problem for dentists and lawyers, sex is a problem for surgeons and therapists and psychiatrists. And sex is a problem for Scott Peck.

In my vision of this world as a kind of celestial boot camp—replete with obstacles that have been almost fiendishly designed for our learning—of all the obstacles that God designed for our learning, I think the one that He or She most fiendishly designed is sex. God built into us a feeling that we can solve the problem of sex and be forever sexually fulfilled, that we can get over the obstacle. Indeed, for a couple of weeks or a couple of months, or maybe even for a couple of years, if we are lucky, we may feel that we have solved the problem of sex. But then, of course, we change or our partners change, or the whole ball game changes, and once again we are left trying to scramble over that obstacle with this built-in feeling that we can get over it, when actually we never can.

However, in the process of trying to get over it, we

learn a great deal about vulnerability and intimacy and love and how to whittle away at our narcissism. Some of us even get to graduate from boot camp. And if you involve God in the process, the chances of success improve, and to do that you don't have to be a monk or a nun.

I have come up with my own definitions of celibacy and chastity. I arrived at these definitions thinking about the times when I was "on the make." That is the appropriate expression, because what I was trying to do was to make sex happen. I would have it all plotted out. I would take the woman who was the object of my desire out to dinner at a nice restaurant, and then to a movie, and then back to my apartment, where I would have tapes and records all picked out, and then we would go to bed. That's how I was going to make it happen. But contrary to my best-laid plans, I usually couldn't make it happen, and occasionally when I did, it wasn't a particularly great experience.

Some of the most glorious sexual experiences I ever had, however, were the ones that not only seemed just to happen but also seemed to be orchestrated by angels off in the wings—specifically, not by me. So I got to thinking that chastity maybe should be defined as a three-way relationship between two human beings and God, in which God is allowed to call the shots.

If you were to define chastity in that way, then there are a number of implications. One is that chastity is much harder than celibacy, which I define simply as the decision to refrain from sexual activity, at least for a period of time. Another is that chastity is filled with traps because it's extraordinarily easy for us to convince ourselves that God wants us to do what we are doing. Still another implication is that it is possible for premarital or extramarital sex to be quite chaste. And conversely, that it is possible for marital sex to be profoundly unchaste.

When I was practicing psychotherapy, I sometimes suggested to married couples whose sex had gotten perfunctory that they might want to experiment with periods of chastity. Chastity and celibacy are two valid options for at least some people. And I think I would have made that suggestion even if I were a secular psychiatrist and not a religious one, because of several experiences I have had.

One was a number of years ago. I was working with a young woman, a Ph.D. schooled at the best universities, and among her many symptoms was a compulsive need to engage in sexual relationships which she neither desired nor enjoyed. We went through all the usual Freudian psychodynamics trying to get to the root of this symptom without any success, until one day I asked her, "You don't happen to believe, do you, that a very active sex life is a necessary part of mental health?" And she said, "Well of course. I mean, isn't that the way it is?"

The poor woman felt that she had to compulsively engage in sexual relationships which she neither desired nor enjoyed simply to maintain an image of herself as mentally healthy. What an extraordinary relief it was for her when, after she had abstained from sex for three weeks, I gave her a certificate of mental health.

I have seen the same phenomenon among elderly couples. In the past dozen years or so, there has been a whole spate of articles in the psychiatric and psychological literature saying that it is really pretty normal for elderly people to have sexual relationships. However, as with any kind of change in outlook, I'm always worried a little bit about the pendulum swinging too far. I am concerned that now that we professionals have so graciously given the elderly permission to have sex, we may start telling them they should have it whether they like it or not—in order to stay young, or something.

In the course of my career, I have run into two elderly couples who were deeply in love with each other, yet in both instances each partner confessed to me individually, in private, that he or she had lost sexual interest in the other, or in anyone else for that matter. They were continuing to have a sexual relationship, however, because each felt that the other partner wanted it. So I got the two of them together, brought this out in the open, and suggested, "Since neither of you wants sex, why don't you stop?" It was like a veritable revelation to them. They had never considered that it was all right to stop.

I am reminded of that famous passage from Ecclesiastes which begins, "To every thing there is a season, and a time to every purpose under the heaven," and goes on to say, "A time to embrace, and a time to refrain from embracing." This is profound secular as well as spiritual wisdom. Sex is a great gift, but that doesn't necessarily mean that it is a gift to be picked up by all people at all times in all seasons.

GOD AND SEX

In any discussion of sex, the notion of a sexual relationship between human beings and God is likely to be the most controversial and shocking. While I think that almost everyone would accept that the most passionate relationships we can have with God are romantic ones, they would question whether sex or sexuality is actually involved. Most people would maintain that the erotic poetry of the Bible or of people like Saint John of the Cross is no more than a poetic metaphor for a passionate spirituality. At most they might agree with Alan Jones, who said that sexual love is a robust symbol of a yet more robust love. I think there is some truth in this. But I do not think it is the whole truth.

Shocking as it may seem, I think there *is* a genuine sexual element in the relationship between human beings and God. What this means, if I am correct, is not only that we human beings are sexual creatures, but also that God is in fact a sexual being. That is hardly what I have always believed. When I was in college, my favorite quote was one from Voltaire: "If God created us in His own image, we have certainly returned the compliment." Nothing seemed more absurd to me than imagining God in anthropomorphic terms, as an old man with a long white beard or a being with genitalia. It seemed to me that God must be infinitely different and infinitely more than we can possibly imagine Him or Her to be. And so He or She is.

However, in the years since college, I have also come to realize that the very deepest means we have to even begin to comprehend something about the nature of God is through a projection onto Him or Her of the very best of our human nature. And that God—among other things and above all other things—is *humane*. He represents humanity at its best, which has something to do with what is meant by God creating us in His own image.

GOD AS A SEDUCER

I believe that God not only created us in His own image but continues to do so. And I am indebted to the Episcopal theologian and author Robert Capon for pointing out the obvious logic that since God created us in His own image, and since we are sexual creatures, it might only stand to reason that God is a sexual being.

One reason that this syllogism makes sense to me, in addition to its logic, is that I myself have experienced God as a seducer. Substitute another word in your mind, like "lover" or "wooer," if you will, but obviously God has succeeded in seducing me, although more often than not I have run away from Him like a frightened, reluctant virgin. Once again, in Capon's words, this sexy God's love for us is profoundly seductive—"He is a God who is continually on the make."

God could have made sex as secular as breathing or eating. But instead He brushed it with a spiritual flavor, and He did this very deliberately, I think, in order to give us a taste for Him. Because above all else, He wants to lure us to Him. This notion of God not only as a sexual being but as a particularly seductive one is perhaps somewhat supportive of our traditional masculine image of Him. Certainly He does behave with an aggressiveness in the hunt that we have typically associated with males. I think that this association itself is sexist and I have met a few good huntresses in my time. But in any case, as Francis Thompson's famous poem "The Hound of Heaven" suggests, He chases after us with a vigor that is matched only by the vigor with which we may flee from Him. And when we are finally caught, we may experience our conversion, as I suggested in *The Road Less Traveled*, not necessarily as an "Oh joy!" phenomenon, but often as an "Oh shit!" phenomenon. Because we have been trapped. Because we have been brought to bay. Because we have finally and irrevocably been caught.

That's what it's all about. Not that He is male, not that She is female—He/She is both and more—but that He is after us, that He wants us, that He loves us beyond belief, and that He intends to have us, no matter how fast and far we flee. And our individual struggle is only over how long we are going to stick with our prudish little hang-ups and our narcissistic little reticences before we finally and willingly open ourselves in surrender to Him. As John Donne did when he wrote his Holy Sonnet XIV:

Batter my heart, three person'd God . .
Take me to you, imprison me, for I,
Except you enthrall me, never shall be free,
Nor ever chaste, except you ravish me.

Psychiatry's Predicament[*]

All of us are agents of history, playing out our roles, shifting or failing to shift according to its tides. And at this moment in history, many feel the need for a shift in American psychiatry. Over the past twenty-five years, American psychiatry has increasingly run with the "medical model"—namely, a model which places far greater emphasis on the distinctly materialistic and biological aspects of psychiatric disease than on other aspects. It is in no way my intent to disparage the profound biochemical advances that have been made over the past forty years in the treatment and understanding of mental illness, or to discourage future progress in this area. Nonetheless, along with many, I am concerned that psychiatry, in its recent enamoredness with biochemistry, may be in grave danger of losing all its old psychological and social wisdom, as well as of failing to gain any new wisdom on these fronts.

It is not an idle concern. In 1987, a colleague and I examined a candidate for certification by the American

[*] Adapted from an address as Distinguished Psychiatrist Lecturer to the American Psychiatric Association on May 4, 1992, in Washington. D. C.

Board of Psychiatry and Neurology. He was a highly intelligent man in his late thirties who possessed at least as much compassion as the other candidates. However, when asked by my colleague to give a psychodynamic formulation of the case in question, he replied, "I don't do psychodynamics." A certain shift or correction might seem to be in order.

Indeed, I believe we need to explore the possibility of an even greater shift. Although perhaps recently underestimated, the psychodynamic and social aspects of mental illness have held a respected place in the history of American psychiatry. Its spiritual aspects, however, have not. Psychiatry has not only neglected but actively ignored the issue of spirituality.

Contributing to this situation is the fact that the topic of spirituality is so subject to misinterpretation. In part, this is due to a poverty in our language. Throughout the world, there is confusion between the terms "spirituality" and "religion." Many identify the term "religion" with organized religion and a system of dogma and sanctions with which they have often had unfortunate experience. It is a hot-button word. There is even disagreement about the meaning of its Latin root, *religio*, which has been variously translated as "restrain," "reliance," or "connection"—all very different concepts.

The classic turn-of-the-century work by the great American psychologist William James, *The Varieties of Religious Experience*, is mandatory first-year reading for most divinity students and unread by most students of psychiatry. In it, James defined religion as "the attempt to be in harmony with an unseen order of things." He was using "religion" in its sense of "to connect." I will use it here as my definition of spirituality. The attempt to be in harmony with an unseen order does not imply a preference for any one doctrine over another or the necessity for membership in any particular organization.

It is my own faith—call it a theory, if you so choose—that there is indeed an unseen order of things behind the veil of materialism. And not only is it proper that humans attempt to be in harmony with that order, but also that the unseen order is actually and actively attempting to be in harmony with us. One consequence of this faith is my belief that everyone has a spiritual life, just as they have an unconscious, whether they like it or not. That many ignore, actively deny, or vigorously flee from the unseen order doesn't mean they are not spiritual beings; it only means they are trying to avoid the fact. Others may think of themselves as atheists and deny the existence of God, yet they passionately believe that things like truth, beauty, and social justice are very much a part of an unseen order, and dedicate themselves to such an unseen order with a passion far greater than that of most who regularly attend a church, synagogue, mosque, or temple. Thus, we are all spiritual beings, and I believe that a psychiatry which does not regard humans as spiritual beings may be largely missing the boat.

In discussing the topic of spirituality, I hope I do not strip it of all its power and poetry. For some of us, myself included, the essence of the unseen order is God, and God should not be taken lightly. A Hasidic story passed on to me by Erich Fromm makes the point. It is the story of a good Jewish man—let us call him Mordecai—who prayed one day, "O God, let me know Your true name, even as the angels do." The Lord God heard his prayer and granted it, allowing Mordecai to know

His true name. Whereupon Mordecai crept under the bed and yelped in sheer animal terror, "O God, let me forget Your true name." And the Lord God heard that prayer and granted it also. Something of the same point was made by the Apostle Paul when he said, "It is a terrifying thing to fall into the hands of the living God."

I do not pretend to know the true name of God. I see enormous virtue in the wording of the third step of AA and the other twelve-step programs: "Make a decision to turn our will and our lives over to the care of God *as we understand Him.*" I would only alter the phrase to "as we understand Him or Her." Henceforth, I will perhaps be more dispassionate, but only having made the point that we are touching on holy ground.

Psychiatry has its own power. For instance, during my training in the mid-sixties when psychiatry was more broad-based—more bio-psycho-social—than it is today, I was taught a terribly important principle: "All symptoms are overdetermined." It is a principle which many other physicians, theologians, scholars, and most lay people desperately need to learn. In any case, I believe the failure of American psychiatry to deal with the issue of spirituality is itself a profoundly overdetermined symptom rooted in multiple historical forces and other factors. Five of them seem more important to me than any others.

Far and away the most important and deepest root of our current predicament extends back long before Freud, long before Philippe Pinel and Benjamin Rush and the existence of "modern" psychiatry. Prior to the seventeenth century, the relationship between science and religion was primarily one of integration. That integration was known as philosophy. The early philosophers—men like Plato, Aristotle, and Thomas Aquinas—were of scientific bent, thinking in terms of evidence and questioning premises, but they were also utterly convinced that God, as they understood Him, was the central reality. By the beginning of the seventeenth century, however, things had begun to go sour, coming to a head in 1633 when Galileo was summoned before the Inquisition. In order to deal with the fallout from such events—in order to smooth the waters between science and religion— near the end of the seventeenth century, an unwritten social contract was developed, divvying up the territory between science, religion, and government. Peace was achieved by giving each its own turf. With minor exceptions, government was not supposed to interfere with science or with religion. Religion was not supposed to interfere with government or science. And science was not supposed to interfere with religion or government. All manner of good came from this unwritten contract.

But in the last half of the twentieth century, it is becoming increasingly obsolete, and a new and very different kind of contract is beginning to be drawn in virtually all spheres of human activity. What is going on in psychiatry is only a small part of the big picture. The influence of American psychiatry on human intellectual life during the past ninety years has been far greater than the number of psychiatrists might imply. But if American psychiatry fails to shift with the new tide, it is likely to end up in an intellectual backwater.

Let us consider the roles of science and religion under the old unwritten contract. In the early 1700s, Isaac Newton was president of the Royal Society of London for Improving Natural Knowledge. Under the old contract, then already in place, natural knowledge was distinguished from supernatural knowledge. "Natural knowledge" was the province of science, "supernatural knowledge" was the province of religion, and according to the rules of the old contract, never the twain should meet. One effect of that separation was the emasculation of philosophy. Since natural knowledge became the province of the scientists and supernatural knowledge the province of the theologians, the poor philosophers were left only with what fell through the cracks, which was not much. Philosophy eventually became a relatively arcane and totally elective subject in our colleges. The most visible remnant of its once glorious past is in outmoded titles which have their origin in the Middle Ages. So it is today that a graduate student, after some years of study and research in the field of microbiology, will be awarded for his or her efforts a doctor of philosophy degree, even though she or he may never have taken a single philosophy course.

The separation of science and religion also had a profound effect upon the practice of psychotherapy. I was taught—as virtually all psychiatrists are taught—that psychotherapy should somehow be a scientific form of endeavor. An ideal of "pure science" was held before us, and we were admonished that science should be "value-free." It was nonsense, of course. It is not possible to do anything, much less practice psychotherapy, without values. All along, we psychotherapists were operating within a value system so close to us that we were not particularly conscious of it. The name that has been given to that value system is secular humanism.

As for religion specifically, the APA has actual guidelines to the effect that a psychiatrist should not inject religion into treatment when it is counter to the patient's belief system, nor should he or she attempt to discredit the patient's belief system. Those sound like "nice" guidelines—and I would hardly advocate their demolition—but they are woefully incomplete. First of all, they are frequently not followed. The guideline against "attempting to discredit the patient's belief system" is generally interpreted to mean that a religious psychiatrist should not impose his or her religion upon a secular humanist patient. But what about the secular humanist psychiatrist who attempts to impose his or her secular humanism upon a religious patient? That imposition is so frequent as to be almost standard, and is made by large numbers of psychiatrists, overtly or covertly, without their even being aware of it.

Let us take the other side of the coin and suppose that a secular humanist psychiatrist is well aware of his own value system and these guidelines, but is dealing with a patient in psychotherapy whose overtly religious belief system comprises either the outer defense or the core of a psychological fixation. Is the psychiatrist prevented then from questioning or confronting such a belief system? What is appropriate? The fact of the matter is that with three hundred years of historical tradition pronouncing that religion is totally out of their domain, and having been trained in this tradition, psychiatrists are ill-equipped indeed to deal with either religious pathology or religious health. No amount of training will ever be sufficient to ensure that the practitioner never founders. The traditional lack of training in the realm of spirituality, however, assures that most well-trained, astute practitioners will often flounder destructively in these matters.

The second most important determinant, to my

mind—a consequence of the first—for American psychiatry's profound neglect of spirituality is the virtually total ignorance on the part of psychiatrists of the stages of spiritual development. I doubt that it is possible for a psychiatrist to complete his or her residency training without significant exposure to stage theory: to Freud's stages of psychosexual development, to Piaget's stages of cognitive development, and Erikson's stages of maturation and their predictable crises. Yet, to my knowledge, in their training psychiatrists receive absolutely no exposure to the stages of spiritual development. Not the only, but the primary reason for this fact is that psychiatry residency training programs have simply not regarded it as their responsibility to teach anything about spirituality. Indeed, in some respects, they have regarded it as their responsibility *not* to teach anything about spirituality. This extraordinary state of affairs is, of course, the result of that unwritten social contract which allocated the study of spirituality to religion or theology, while psychiatry clearly identified itself with the scientific camp, which was constrained to restrict itself to the study of "natural phenomena."

I have described elsewhere my understanding and interpretation of the stages of spiritual development. In brief, they are: Stage One, which I label chaotic/antisocial and which may be thought of as a stage of lawlessness, absent of spirituality;

Stage Two, which I label formal/institutional and which may be thought of as a rigorous adherence to the letter of the law and attachment to the forms of religion;

Stage Three, which I label skeptic/individual and which is a stage of principled behavior, but one characterized by religious doubt or disinterest, albeit accompanied by inquisitiveness about other areas of life;

And finally Stage Four, the most mature of the stages, which I label mystical/communal and which may be thought of as a state of the spirit of the law, as opposed to Stage Two, which tends to be one of the letter of the law.

You may quickly see parallels between these stages of spiritual development and the psychosexual developmental stages with which psychiatrists are generally familiar—Stage One corresponding in some ways to the first five years of life, Stage Two to the latency period, Stage Three to adolescence and early adulthood, and Stage Four to the last half of life in healthy human development. And like developmental stages, the stages of spiritual development are sequential. They cannot be skipped over, there are people in between stages, and there are gradations within stages.

The diagnosis of the stage into which a particular individual falls needs to be made with some care and discernment. Because a man is a scientist, he may look as if he is in Stage Three, when actually he has a primarily Stage Two spirituality. Another may sell mystical sayings in Stage Four language but actually be a Stage One con artist. Just as there are fixations of psychosexual development, so people may become spiritually fixated in one of these stages, sometimes for some of the same reasons. Finally, let me point out that a small minority may not fit very well into this stage system, but that in itself may be diagnostic. For instance, those we call borderline personalities tend to have a foot in Stage One, a foot in Stage Two, a hand in Stage Three, and a hand in Stage Four—it being no accident that since they are ''borderline,'' they tend to be all over the place.

There are many reasons why an understanding of these stages of spiritual development is critical, but the most important relate to the fact that the vast majority of psychiatrists—including those who are training new psychiatrists—are Stage Three people. As such, on the whole they are more spiritually developed than the majority of churchgoers or those who are identifiably religious. On the other hand, they are less spiritually developed than a minority of the identifiably religious. Ignorance of this reality has profound implications. It predisposes psychiatrists not only to look upon all religion as inferior and pathological, but also to be oblivious to the fact that they themselves may have a spiritual distance to travel.

The third root cause for American psychiatry's neglect of spirituality is the profound influence of Freud. Whatever the reasons, Freud has had a far more profound influence upon American psychiatry than upon psychiatry anywhere else on the globe, with the possible exceptions of Brazil and Argentina. In his native Austria, for instance, he is a figure of relatively minor significance. In the United States he is, even today—and, I believe, deservedly so—a towering figure.

Freud grew up and came into maturity during the heyday of the unwritten social contract separating science and religion. He was a Stage Three individual who completely identified himself with science and was deeply threatened by the issue of spirituality, so much so as to terminate his relationship with his most beloved disciple, Jung.

In 1962, during my training in psychiatry in medical school, we fourth-year students received a brief series of lectures on the history of psychiatry. An entire lecture was devoted to Freud. In another lecture about lesser figures, our professor stated, "And then there is Carl Jung, who received a certain amount of undeserved attention for reasons that are unclear." End of discussion. At that time, many of Freud's writings could be found in the average local bookstore, and none of Jung's. Today, of course, you are likely to find some of Jung's works in the local bookstore and unlikely to find Freud's.

I believe that Freud was the greater psychiatrist, and while he made more mistakes than Jung, he made so many major contributions to psychiatry that we even take them for granted. And while Jung made fewer mistakes and his work is profoundly significant, his contributions have hardly matched those of Freud. He was the lesser psychiatrist. He was also the more spiritually developed individual. This, incidentally, points up the fact that there is no one-to-one correspondence between the importance of the contributions made by individuals and their stage of spiritual development. In any case, the influence of the Stage Three Freud in the United States has further entrenched the secularism of American psychiatry.

The fourth factor that has predisposed American psychiatry to excessive secularism and neglect of spirituality has been the large number of patients we have all seen who have been hurt by religion or in the name of religion. Such experiences have cemented the already overdetermined antipathy of many psychiatrists to religion. And in their antipathy and predisposition, they have generally failed to realize they are dealing with a biased sample of humanity.

Two biases have been involved. The first is that, as physicians, we tend to see the diseased, the casualties.

We see people who have been hurt by rigid, frigid nuns or else by their early Stage Two, destructively dogmatic, fundamentalist Protestant parents. We are less likely to see people such as Babe Ruth and Ethel Waters, who were dramatically rescued or saved from antisocial Stage One childhoods by supposedly rigid, frigid nuns.

The second bias affecting psychiatrists specializing in psychotherapy has been patient self-selection. Many patients have gravitated to Stage Three secular psychotherapists precisely because they themselves have already begun their spiritual journey out of Stage Two and primitive religion into skepticism and individuation.

One of the most important reasons it is so critical to understand the stages of spiritual development is because of the sense of threat that exists between people in different stages, and their inevitable interaction in the therapeutic setting. There is a profound tendency for us human beings to look up to someone who is one step— perhaps a third of a stage—ahead of us as a wise person or guru. On the other hand, if someone is two steps ahead of us, we usually think that he or she is a threat, even evil. That is what happened to Socrates and Jesus. This means that the most spiritually developed people do not necessarily make the best therapists for everyone. Rather, it is Stage Two people and rigid programs that often offer the best therapy for Stage One people. Stage Three people—a role that has been played by secular psychotherapists—often serve as the best guides for people moving out of Stage Two. And Stage Four people make the best therapists for those in the further reaches of Stage Three or spiritual directors for those who have already entered Stage Four. In any case, secular therapists have tended to be sought out by those who have already begun to identify Stage Two formulistic religious thinking as a destructive influence in their lives and something they are at least partially ready to outgrow.

The fifth and final determinant of American psychiatry's prevailing antipathy toward spirituality has been the profound distrust and suspicion of psychiatry by many Stage Two religious people. This antipathy has often been unjustified, and is a function not of realistic thinking but of the sense of threat that exists between people in different stages of spiritual development. Many fundamentalist Christians, for example, have ascribed psychiatry—along with evolution and world government—to the devil.

I have had personal experience with the sense of threat that exists among both Stage Two religious people and Stage Three secular people. For over a decade, without any success, I have tried to encourage the development of what I call an Institute for the Scientific Study of Deliverance, defining deliverance as any form of healing in which deities are invoked, and which can range from such extremely common phenomena as prayer healing through deliverance—a form of mini-exorcism routinely practiced by fundamentalist Christians—all the way to full-scale "combative" exorcism. Only once did it look as if I might possibly succeed in this endeavor.

Ten years ago I worked with the chairman of the board of a large psychiatric center. The center consisted of two parts. One was a 120-bed inpatient unit led primarily by Stage Three secular scientific-minded psychiatrists; the other was a large outpatient service led primarily by Stage Two religiously oriented pastoral counselors. In the forty years of the center's existence, these two parts of the organization had been almost armed camps at dramatic odds with each other. The chairman of the board thought that my proposed institute might be something that could bring these two hostile factions together. He was correct. They came together in opposition to my proposal. The secular psychiatrists said that my operational definitions were too fuzzy, there were too many variables, and the whole field was inherently unresearchable. The religious nurses and pastoral counselors said that everyone knows that prayer works, and you shouldn't tamper with faith. So it was that the first time in forty years that these two armed camps came together was to oppose the scientific study of spiritual phenomena.

American psychiatry is, I believe, currently in a predicament. I call it a predicament because its traditional neglect of the issue of spirituality has led to five broad areas of failure: occasional, devastating misdiagnosis; not infrequent mistreatment; an increasingly poor reputation; inadequate research and theory; and a limitation of psychiatrists' own personal development. Taken further, these failures are so destructive to psychiatry that the predicament can properly be called grave.

In the category of misdiagnosis are the cases in which otherwise competent psychiatrists routinely ignore or distort the spiritual aspects of their patients' lives so as either to totally miss the diagnosis or to make a diagnosis which is harmfully incomplete. To illustrate this area of failure, I offer two clinical vignettes from my personal experience over the past nine years—a period when I have hardly been in practice at all.

The earliest occurred in the winter of 1983, when I had already largely wound down my practice but was still doing some consulting. I was phoned by a man requesting my consultation in the case of his sixty-four-year-old wife, who had been hospitalized for the preceding three years in one of the most prestigious psychiatric hospitals in the nation. From the husband I learned of the very sudden onset of devastating psychosis at the age of sixty in a woman who for the entirety of her life had apparently been mentally completely healthy and, for almost forty years, an ideally functioning, perfectly stable wife, mother, grandmother, and member of the community. Upon questioning, however, I did spot a red flag.

Three years prior to the sudden onset of psychosis, this woman, who had been a lifelong and active member of the Presbyterian church, had suddenly, without any explanation to her husband or others, left that traditional denomination and joined the Unity church, a far more liberal Christian church (indeed, so liberal that some would consider it to be heretical—a bit of a New Age church). I also learned that she had become extremely close to the younger and very charismatic minister of this new church.

A month later I went to the hospital to see the woman in consultation. I spent half an hour with her personally. She was well kept, polite, and proper. She was oriented times three. She did not appear depressed. In our brief time together, I was not able to arrive at my own diagnosis. The only thing I could say with certainty was that she was both facilely and profoundly evasive about her personal life and, particularly, her spiritual life. Our meeting was so brief because she insisted that it end when I confronted her with her evasiveness.

I spent much time reviewing her records. She had been variously diagnosed as having depression, involutional psychotic depression, bipolar disease manifested by depression, possible schizophrenia, and possible chronic organic brain syndrome. Over the course of her three years in the hospital, she had failed utterly to respond to antidepressants, phenothiazines, and electroshock therapy, or even to respond to or become engaged in psychotherapy. Reluctantly, her psychiatrist acknowledged that they were unsure of what diagnostic category to put her in. There was no mention in her records of a spiritual history, much less her sudden change in denominations three years before the onset of her psychosis. Nor were the psychiatrists then in charge of her case aware of any spiritual history or this particular red flag. I recommended an intensive psychodynamic diagnostic intervention process that would include spiritual consultation. My recommendation was not acted upon, on the grounds that a lengthier stay in the hospital was unsupportable. The woman was transferred to a nursing home, and my further services were not sought.

I cannot tell you that woman's diagnosis. What I can tell you, however, is that in the course of three years of unbelievably expensive treatment in this most prestigious, traditional psychiatric hospital, a patient's spiritual life had been utterly overlooked and no adequate diagnosis had been formulated. I will go further and state that no adequate diagnosis had even been attempted in a case where the traditional diagnostic rubrics did not seem to fit.

The second case is that of a young man I never saw. He was a patient of a highly competent, secular psychiatrist—Ted, I will call him—who had been a friend of mine in medical school. In 1989, happening to be lecturing in his city, I dined with him and had the opportunity to catch up on the twenty-five years since we had last met. I learned that he had come to specialize in the treatment of multiple-personality disorder. He was particularly excited about a young man he was currently treating, in whom he had, to date, uncovered some fifty-two different personalities, one of which, he commented as an aside, "calls himself Judas—and he's a real bad guy."

I asked Ted whether he ever had the feeling that his patient was "toying" with him. "No," Ted responded. "Why do you ask?" I suggested the possibility that he might have a case of possession on his hands—either one coexisting with multiple-personality disorder or possibly even one for which the MPD was a sham. With his secular orientation, Ted wouldn't even consider my suggestion. I left feeling sad at what seemed to me a significant possibility—if not probability—that my otherwise competent friend was misdiagnosing and hence mistreating his most intensive case at the time. And that he was utterly immune to even my gentlest consultation on the matter.

Misdiagnosis almost inevitably results in mistreatment. But that is hardly the end of it, because mistreatment or inadequate treatment can occur in the face of a correct diagnosis. Indeed, my concern with misdiagnosis is relatively minor. A far greater problem, to my mind, has been the vast amount of mistreatment of patients with a correct primary diagnosis by virtue of psychiatry's neglect of and antipathy for spiritual issues. This kind of mistreatment generally falls into one or more of five categories: failure to listen, denigration of the patient's humanity, failure to encourage healthy spirituality, failure to combat unhealthy spirituality or false theology, and failure to comprehend important aspects of the patient's life.

The single most common complaint I hear from psychotherapy patients about their therapists (they are just as likely to be secular-minded psychologists and social workers as psychiatrists, but psychiatry has tended to call the tune) has been that they did not or would not listen to the spiritual aspects of their lives. When patients talk about such things as a feeling of calling, consideration of entering monastic life or the ministry, mystical experiences, or even simple belief in God, the prevailing tendency of psychotherapists is to simply shut down until the patients are speaking of more mundane matters—or else to actively attempt to divert them to more mundane matters. Many patients have left therapists as a result.

Even more common is that the patient, picking up on the therapist's cues, will enter into a kind of unspoken collusion where both agree to avoid spiritual issues. Typically, patients will tell me, "I really like my therapist. He [or she] is a decent person. I feel he is trying to help me, and indeed, he has been of some help. But you wouldn't believe how threatened he gets whenever I mention the spiritual side of my life. So, since I'm getting some help, I've learned to simply hide that side of my life from him and never mention it. But I sure wish it could be different. I wish I could be wholly myself in his office. Sometimes I think I would be better off with a therapist who is more receptive, but at the moment it doesn't seem worth the trouble to start all over again. And besides, I'm not that far away from termination. But if I ever go back into therapy, I'm certainly going to look for a more broad-minded therapist.''

I have also heard a significant number of stories of therapists who have actively denigrated their patients' spiritual life. This is not to say that a person's spirituality is always healthy and should never be confronted, but my impression of these cases is that the therapist involved was unable to discern between a healthy and an unhealthy spirituality.

Of even deeper concern to me, however, is a more general denigration of the humanity of psychiatric patients. Let me provide an example. I have had the unusual opportunity of seeing one schizophrenic patient roughly twice a year over the course of the past eighteen years. When I first saw her in consultation at a local clinic, she was in her early thirties, suffering from suspiciousness, frequent periods of depression and apathy, fleeting delusions, social isolation, and grave difficulty in sustaining either employment or social relations. Additionally, she demonstrated profound ambivalence, flattening of affect, and extreme social maladeptness. Shortly after I first saw her, she was placed on Social Security disability and has remained on it ever since.

When I left my consulting position at the clinic, she continued to drop by my home twice a year for a free visit of fifteen to thirty minutes. Today, at age fifty, she demonstrates all the signs of moderate, well-entrenched, chronic schizophrenia. The course of her disease over eighteen years has been consistent and stable. From a traditional psychiatric point of view, she has neither deteriorated nor made any progress whatsoever. It would be easy to regard her as a chronic lost cause. However, over the course of those years, she has moved from skepticism to a tentative interest in religion to a deep faith. She now attends Mass at least weekly. Her theology is not in the least bizarre; it is, as best I can ascertain, not only traditional and sound but quite sophisticated. In return for my extremely minor ministrations, she regularly prays for me. I think I have, by far, the better part of the bargain. Many would regard hers as a wasted sort of life in which there has been no progress. From my point of view, while there has been no improvement in her schizophrenia or growth in her social skills, there has been immense growth in her soul. Something very profound has slowly been happening within her.

When we psychiatrists do not know how to help those with a chronic mental illness such as schizophrenia, we have a tendency to write them off. We also do this with mental retardation and, even more so, with such conditions as senility. Yet I have seen patients who have been correctly diagnosed with Alzheimer's disease who have made considerable spiritual strides in their lives since that diagnosis.

Since psychiatrists are generally unable to distinguish between a healthy and an unhealthy spirituality, they are generally unable to align themselves with a healthy one and support it. A bright spot on the horizon has been the appearance of several recent articles in the professional literature by therapists offering clinical vignettes of how their patients' treatment seemed to be clearly enhanced or speeded up by the encouragement of their seemingly healthy religious activity or spiritual belief system.

Another reason for either misdiagnosis or mistreatment or both through psychiatrists' ignorance of theology and the realm of spirituality is their failure to spot false ideas, false thinking, or, in religious terms, heresies. You may think—as I once did—that heresy is a subject properly belonging back in the days of the Inquisition or the Middle Ages, but I can assure you that heresy is very much alive and well at the end of the twentieth century and adversely affecting millions of individuals as well as society as a whole. Much heresy arises when people run with just one side of a paradox in their thinking. And heresies, being at best half-truths, are essentially lies.

Another effect of misdiagnosis or, more commonly, mistreatment resulting from the avoidance or disparagement of spirituality has been a significant deterioration in the reputation of psychiatry and psychiatrists. The word is out. Large numbers of people steer clear of the psychotherapy that psychiatrists have to offer because they have heard of psychiatry's antipathy to spirituality. This, in turn, has encouraged the competition. Sometimes competition can be good. It is no accident that pastoral counseling has been one of the most rapidly growing career fields over the course of the past twenty-five years. The first pastoral counseling training program was established in 1948. There are now approximately two hundred such programs. Many of them, as best I can ascertain, are very good. And many pastoral counselors are doing superb work. Indeed, unless a patient has a severe psychiatric disturbance clearly suggesting pharmacotherapy in addition to psychotherapy, I am probably more likely to refer him or her to a pastoral counselor than to a psychiatrist.

But not all competition is healthy. In reaction to psychiatry's failure to deal with spiritual issues over the past decade, there has been an explosive expansion of Christian fundamentalist treatment programs, on the one hand, and what I choose to call New Age fundamentalist practitioners, on the other. I have reason to question the healthiness of this kind of competition from the fringes. But if it is unhealthy competition, it exists largely by traditional psychiatry's default.

Psychiatry's dis-ease with spirituality has also resulted in a significant failure of both research and theory. A tiny amount of research in the area of spirituality and religion has been undertaken at Harvard and a few other places, but it is minuscule compared to the need. And psychiatry is not the only villain involved. As I noted, religion has as much reluctance to subject spirituality to real research as does psychiatry.

It is hardly remarkable that where a dearth of research exists, there is also going to be a stagnation of theory. Perhaps I suffer from being out of the mainstream. From my vantage point, however, as far as I can ascertain, the most significant contributions to personality theory and psychodynamic theory over the past generation have not been made by psychiatrists; they have been made by pastoral counselors, by management consultants and industrial psychologists, and by theologians and poets. Perhaps the most serious aspect of psychiatry's predicament is that by ignoring their own spirituality as individuals—and by being taught by their mentors to so ignore it—psychiatrists themselves are placing severe limitations upon their psychospiritual development.

Fifteen years ago my wife, Lily, and I had the opportunity to consult with a convent as an organization. The consultation was requested because many of the nuns were suffering from disorders which were, quite obviously, psychosomatic, and the community did not know how to deal with the situation. Over and over again, Lily and I kept saying to the twenty or so gathered together in the Mother House, "Look, you are a highly educated group of people, many of you with doctorates, who are specialists in love and healing. If any group of people ought to have the capacity to deal with each other about such issues, you should." But they didn't buy it. Over and over again, they kept rebutting, "But we're not professionals. We're not trained to discern what is physical and what is psychological, what is psychological and what is spiritual." For twenty-four hours we were at an absolute impasse, until a novice suddenly blurted out, "If I hear you correctly, what being a psychotherapist means—and doing psychotherapy—is essentially working on oneself." We exclaimed in return, "You've got it." The consultation was a success.

So I would hold that the essential characteristic of a psychiatrist's development is her, or his, capacity to work on herself. But what to work on? If she does not regard herself as being on a spiritual journey, it seems to me that the work is likely to be merely intellectual and probably arid. On the other hand, if she can accept—embrace—the idea that she is on a spiritual journey, then it is highly likely that such self-work will be rich and rewarding, not only for herself but for her patients. There are enormous ambiguities involved. For instance, she may outgrow her patients. She may even leave the practice of psychiatry for strange new fields. But the overall result, I suggest, is that her journey will be more fruitful both to herself and to those she treats. Conversely, should she deny that she herself has a spiritual life, I suspect that her own development will be narrow and also that of her patients.

* * *

273

Although the predicament of psychiatry is, I believe, grave, the treatment of its condition could be quite simple. I would propose five therapeutic measures. If all of them were undertaken, the problem would be completely taken care of. If even one of them was taken, there would be substantial alleviation of the problem. Three of these proposed five measures would best be implemented within psychiatric residency training and, therefore, the responsibility of such residency–training program directors.

Let me begin with the simplest. I believe that in the first month of their training, all psychiatry residents should be taught to routinely take a spiritual history, just as they are now taught to routinely take a more general history and do a mental status exam.

I made this proposal once to an already spiritually oriented, sixty-year-old man who was chairman of the department of psychiatry at a major university medical center. He asked, "What on earth is a spiritual history?" I explained it was a process of asking the patient rather simple and obvious questions: "What religion were you raised in? What denomination? Are you still in that same religion? The same denomination? If not, what religion do you adhere to, and how did the change come about? Are you an atheist? An agnostic? If you are a believer, what is your notion of God? Does God seem abstract and distant, or does God seem close to you and personal? Has this changed recently? Do you pray? What is your prayer life like? Have you had any spiritual experiences? What were they? What effect did they have upon you?" And so on. Six weeks later, the chairman wrote to me saying, "I took my first spiritual history on a patient the other day, and it was amazing what it revealed."

This is such a simple and obvious remedy we must wonder why it wasn't adopted years ago. But again we are confronted with the extraordinary reluctance of psychiatry to relate to spiritual issues. Do these questions seem too intimate? Have psychiatrists thought they would be too threatening to their patients? The fact of the matter is that such questions are not the least bit threatening to patients. They appreciate being asked and like to answer them. I believe the people who have been threatened are the psychiatrists. As well as improving psychiatric diagnosis and psychotherapeutic treatment, it is possible that this simple remedy of routinely taking a spiritual history might make psychiatrists themselves aware that they have their own spiritual life.

My second recommendation would be that during the course of their three years of training—preferably during the first year—psychiatric residents be taught about the different stages of religious growth or spiritual development. Perhaps only one lecture would be required. A simple synopsis of the work of James Fowler would be sufficient reading. Additionally, however, they should be taught some of the factors that might fixate people in immature or self-destructive spiritual stages— factors that are not necessarily different from those that fixate people in more standardly recognized psychosexual stages.

A major effect of such simple training and teaching would be not only to improve the psychiatrist's diagnostic capacity but also to make him aware that spirituality is something that does develop. And that while he may already have come a good way in his own spiritual life, he may still have a way to go. I believe that this training and awareness would contribute enormously to the ongoing maturation of psycho-therapists.

My third recommendation is that during the three years of their training, psychiatry residents receive at least one lecture on the nature of heresy, false ideas, and false assumptions. I believe the more they familiarize themselves with theology, the more adept they will be at spotting such heresies or lies.

My fourth proposal is a task for the formulators of revisions to *DSM III (Diagnostic and Statistical Manual of Mental Disorders III)* or other future manuals. This proposal is in two parts. First, I suggest that there are at least two new diagnoses of mental disorders that need to be seriously considered for incorporation into the *DSM*. One is the diagnostic category of people whom I have labeled as evil, or people of the lie. One man has recently taken up my own work in this regard and devoted his doctoral dissertation to arguing on behalf of a diagnostic category he entitled ''virulent personality disorder.'' I believe his thesis is compelling and the label appropriate. I further believe that serious consideration needs to be given to the diagnosis of possession, with criteria for distinguishing between it and multiple-personality disorder as well as other conditions (with the understanding that it is possible for a patient to suffer from both multiple-personality disorder and possession).

In addition to these new diagnostic categories, I also believe that consideration should be given to establishing a spiritual axis to our diagnoses, an axis along which the patient's stage of spiritual development would be assessed, along with other spiritual factors—ascertained from a discerning spiritual history—that are relevant to his condition and primary diagnosis.

276

Finally, there is the matter of research. Some research, such as my proposal for an Institute for the Scientific Study of Deliverance, could best be performed under the aegis of a specific, separately funded institute, preferably in conjunction with a university. For instance, among other things, such an institute could serve as an archive and repository for videotapes of exorcisms which students and researchers could see, but only under constraints guaranteeing the confidentiality of such materials. Most research. however, could be done within existing academic departments of psychiatry, focusing on smaller projects. Were psychiatry to enter into the field of spiritual research, I believe we would witness a most exciting and badly needed renaissance of personality theory.

All these proposals could be quite simple in their implementation. The big question is the will to implement them. The treatment of psychiatry's predicament is simple, but is the patient willing? I am convinced the treatment would already have been successfully effected had the patient been willing in the past. Consequently, it seems very clear to me that the kind of treatment I have proposed will be implemented only if psychiatry undergoes a change of attitude toward its own therapy in this regard. Is American psychiatry going to change from a position of disinterest in and resistance to issues of human spirituality to a position of openness and vivacious curiosity?

That question can be answered only by psychiatrists themselves. As such, they are agents of history. American psychiatry has had enormous influence upon the entire intellectual life of our civilization. I do not decry the current medical model as long as it is broad-minded and broadly defined. Over the past generation, however, in running with a medical model that has been remarkably one-dimensional and almost purely materialistic, psychiatrists have increasingly backed themselves into a corner where they are expected to function as mere pill pushers and to leave a deep understanding of the human condition to the theologians and pastoral counselors. Perhaps psychiatry will even decide to get out of the psychotherapy business entirely. Perhaps that would be the proper course. I don't really know. But I do know that psychiatry's influence upon the intellectual life of our civilization is waning.

As a psychiatrist myself, who sees great value in the medical model, who has glimpsed the great beauty of the realm of microscopic anatomy, but who has also personally grown enormously from my frequently blind efforts in the field of psychotherapy, I hope the members of my profession will undergo the historic attitude change I have proposed. I hope that as they deliberate within the depths of their souls as well as their minds, they will choose the role of change by no longer being embarrassed by their own spirituality and by proclaiming humans to be spiritual beings to whom psychiatry can offer not only biochemical adjustment but also at least some measure of spiritual sustenance.

About the Author

M. SCOTT PECK, M.D., is a psychiatrist, diagnostician, management consultant, best-selling author, and a founder of the Foundation for Community Encouragement. He lives in northwestern Connecticut.

Among the titles available are:

GOOD MORNING HOLY SPIRIT
Benny Hinn

CATHOLIC PRAYER BOOK

A GATHERING OF HOPE
Helen Hayes

WORDS TO LOVE BY
Mother Teresa

THE PROPHET
Kahlil Gibran

GIFT FROM THE SEA
Anne Morrow Lindbergh

APPLES OF GOLD
Jo Petty

THE POWER OF POSITIVE THINKING
Norman Vincent Peale

THE ROAD LESS TRAVELED
M. Scott Peck

SOMETHING BEAUTIFUL FOR GOD
Malcolm Muggeridge

PRAYERS AND PROMISES
FOR EVERYDAY
Corrie ten Boom

GETTING THROUGH THE NIGHT
Eugenia Price

THE GRACE AWAKENING
Charles Swindoll

A GRIEF OBSERVED
C. S. Lewis

HOPE FOR THE TROUBLED HEART
Billy Graham

LAUGH AGAIN
Charles Swindoll

MAKING ALL THINGS NEW
Henri J. M. Nouwen

IRREGULAR PEOPLE
Joyce Landorf

AND THE ANGELS WERE SILENT
Max Lucado

PRACTICE OF THE PRESENCE OF GOD
Brother Lawrence

MOTHER ANGELICA'S ANSWERS
NOT PROMISES
Mother Angelica

LOVE IS A GENTLE STRANGER
June Masters Bacher

TO HELP YOU THROUGH
THE HURTING
Marjorie Holmes

GUIDEPOSTS TREASURY OF CHRISTMAS

A BOOK OF ANGELS
Sophy Burnham

LOVE'S SILENT SONG
June Masters Bacher

PEACE, LOVE & HEALING
Bernie S. Siegel

**THREE STEPS FORWARD,
TWO STEPS BACK**
Charles Swindoll

JESUS, THE WORD TO BE SPOKEN
Mother Teresa

RUTH
Lois T. Henderson

NOT I, BUT CHRIST
Corrie ten Boom

WORDS OF CERTITUDE
Pope John Paul II

LYDIA
Lois Henderson

THE WILL OF GOD
Leslie Weatherhead

BOOK OF HOURS
Elizabeth Yates

JEWISH WISDOM
David and Esther Gross

INTRODUCING THE BIBLE
William Barclay

GENESEE DIARY
Henri J. M. Nouwen

BE NOT AFRAID
Alanson Houghton

HOPE AND FAITH FOR TOUGH TIMES
Robert Schuller

WHERE IS GOD WHEN IT HURTS
Philip Yancey

THE GREATEST SALESMAN IN THE WORLD
Og Mandino

GOLDEN TREASURY OF PSALMS AND PRAYERS
Edna Beilenson

REACHING OUT
Henri J. M. Nouwen

WHO NEEDS GOD
Harold Kushner

TWO-PART INVENTION
Madeleine L'Engle

ENCOURAGE ME
Charles Swindoll